SKILLSTUFF

The basic skills activity encyclopedia for teachers

Volume I. Reading

by KIDS' STUFF Author
Imogene Forte

Library of Congress Catalog Card Number: 79-89158
ISBN Number: 0-913916-79-X

WHAT'S IN SKILLSTUFF READING?

The Skillstuff Check List sequentially grouped
in basic skills areas
> . . . Word recognition skills
> . . . Word usage skills
> . . . Comprehension skills
> . . . Reading study skills

Model Activities—one or more for each skill

Teacher Lesson Plans—specific skills objectives, preparation and student directions

Student Worksheets—ready for reproduction and use

Competency Reviews—informal mini achievement tests for each of the four skill areas

And Lots More—teacher yellow pages offering lists and lists of phonics, words, idioms, contractions, abbreviations, analogies, etc.

HOW TO USE SKILLSTUFF READING.

To Teach Basic Reading Skills:
Use the skills check list to find out where kids are and what they need to do (you'll find blank ones ready for reproduction on the back of each section title page).

Select and use activities to meet individual or group needs (the indexed skills check list folowing the Table of Contents will speed up this step).

Use the competency review to determine if and to what extent the skill has been mastered.

Begin planning for the next cycle and start over!

THAT'S WHAT SKILLSTUFF READING IS ALL ABOUT.

—just a quick and easy approach to diagnostic/prescriptive instruction in basic reading skills.

> . . .and to add flair and excitement unique to your very own teaching style, use all yellow page goodies to design more and better games, worksheets and individual and group tests and projects.

ACKNOWLEDGMENTS

Special acknowledgment is gratefully accorded

... to Eleanor L. Dunn, Robert J. Shaffer and Mary Ann Pangle for researching and organizing many of the lists found in the Teacher's Yellow Pages section,

... to Mary Hamilton who illustrated the book and to Gayle Seaburg Harvey whose artistic flair contributed to the cover and the section title pages,

... and to Elaine Raphael, editor, critic and contributor, my appreciation is boundless.

TABLE OF CONTENTS

Page

COMPREHENSION SKILLS

SKILLSTUFF: READING CHECKLIST

Student's Name	Grade	Date	Teacher's Name

I. WORD RECOGNITION SKILLS	SKILLSTUFF Activities

PHONETIC ANALYSIS

____ Knows and uses long and short vowels, vowel teams and vowel rules	17, 18, 19, 20, 32
____ Knows and uses consonant sounds, blends and rules	21, 22, 23, 24, 25, 32
____ Recognizes and understands functions of word endings and letter combinations that can be combined to form or change sound and/or meaning of words	26, 27, 28, 29, 30, 31, 45
____ Knows and can use phonetic symbols	32, 33
____ Recognizes rhyming words	34, 35, 36, 37, 38, 39

STRUCTURAL ANALYSIS

____ Knows and can use rules for syllabication	40, 41, 42, 43, 44
____ Recognizes and can expand root words	45
____ Knows and can use prefixes and suffixes	46, 47
____ Can use contractions and abbreviations	48, 49, 50
____ Can use compound words	51, 52, 53, 54, 55
____ Can discriminate between words that look similar but are pronounced differently	58
____ Can interpret plurals and possessives	56, 57

II. WORD USAGE SKILLS   SKILLSTUFF Activities

WORD MEANING

____ Can use sight vocabulary   63, 64, 65

____ Can use picture clues   66, 67

____ Can use context clues   68, 69, 70, 71

____ Can define words by classification or
function   72, 73, 74

____ Can understand multiple meanings of a
given word   75

____ Recognizes and can use common synonyms,
antonyms and homonyms for familiar words   76, 77, 78, 79, 80

____ Recognizes and can use key words in
content areas   81, 82, 83

____ Can interpret and convey meanings of a
variety of familiar words.   84, 85, 86, 87

WORD SENSITIVITY

____ Can associate words with feelings   88, 89, 90, 91

____ Can form sensory impressions   92, 100, 101

____ Can interpret figurative and idiomatic
expressions   93

____ Can interpret sensations and moods suggested by words   94, 95, 96

____ Can recognize word relationships   97, 98, 99

____ Can recognize and use descriptive words   100, 101

____ Is developing word appreciation   102, 103, 104, 105, 106

III. COMPREHENSION SKILLS	SKILLSTUFF Activities
____ Can recall information read and select facts to remember	111
____ Can read for a specific purpose	112, 113
____ Can find the main idea	114, 115, 116
____ Can read to find details	117
____ Can make comparisons and associations	118, 119, 120
____ Can classify material read	121, 122, 123
____ Can arrange ideas or events in sequence	124, 125
____ Can summarize	126, 127, 128, 129
____ Can read to verify answers	130, 131
____ Can draw conclusions	132, 133, 134, 135
____ Can make inferences	136
____ Can predict outcomes	137
____ Can make value judgments	138
____ Can distinguish between	
____ relevant and irrelevant	139
____ fact and opinion	140, 141, 142, 143
____ cause and effect	144, 145
____ Is sensitive to author's purpose and mood	146
____ Can identify with fictional characters	147
____ Can identify character traits	148, 149
____ Is sensitive to the development of plot and sequence	150, 151, 152, 153
____ Can visualize	154, 155, 156

____ Can use the dictionary   161

   ____ alphabetize   162, 163

   ____ use guide words, symbols and keys   164, 165, 166

____ Can determine what reference source to use and use multiple resources related to one topic   167, 168, 169

   ____ thesaurus and encyclopedia   170, 171, 172, 173

   ____ library materials   176

   ____ catalogs, magazines and newspapers   174, 175, 177

   ____ table of contents, index and glossary   178, 179, 180, 181

____ Can read and use systematically organized materials   182

   ____ maps and globes   183, 184, 185

   ____ charts, tables, graphs and diagrams   186, 187, 188, 189

____ Can understand and use punctuation   190, 191

____ Can follow written directions   192, 193, 194, 195

____ Can outline material read   196, 197

____ Can take notes from reading   198

____ Can skim to locate facts and details   199

____ Can organize facts to support a conclusion   200, 201

____ Is developing increased reading rate, accuracy and independence   202, 203, 204, 205, 206

SKILLSTUFF

Word Recognition Skills

SKILLSTUFF: READING CHECKLIST

_____ _____ _____ _____
Student's Name   Grade   Date   Teacher's Name

SKILLSTUFF Activities

I. WORD RECOGNITION SKILLS

PHONETIC ANALYSIS

____ Knows and uses long and short vowels, vowel teams and vowel rules

____ Knows and uses consonant sounds, blends and rules

____ Recognizes and understands functions of word endings and letter combinations that can be combined to form or change sound and/or meaning of words

____ Knows and can use phonetic symbols

____ Recognizes rhyming words

STRUCTURAL ANALYSIS

____ Knows and can use rules for syllabication

____ Recognizes and can expand root words

____ Knows and can use prefixes and suffixes

____ Can use contractions and abbreviations

____ Can use compound words

____ Can discriminate between words that look similar but are pronounced differently

____ Can interpret plurals and possessives

MAIL-A-SOUND

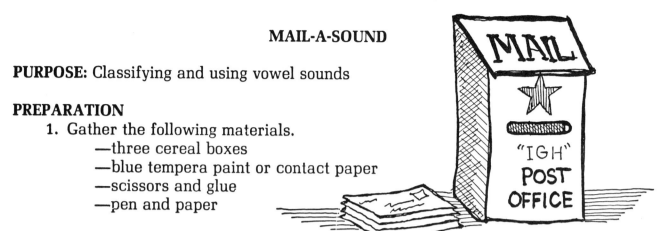

PURPOSE: Classifying and using vowel sounds

PREPARATION
1. Gather the following materials.
   —three cereal boxes
   —blue tempera paint or contact paper
   —scissors and glue
   —pen and paper

2. Make three mail boxes from the cereal boxes. Fix the box tops so they can be closed but will be easy to open. Paint the boxes with blue tempera paint, or cover with blue contact paper and decorate to look like mail boxes. Cut a hole in the front of each box so that envelopes may be deposited in them.

3. On one box, print "-ie;" on the second box, print "-y;" and on the third, print "-igh."

4. Print the following words (or other words with the appropriate vowel sounds) on plain white envelopes (one word per envelope).

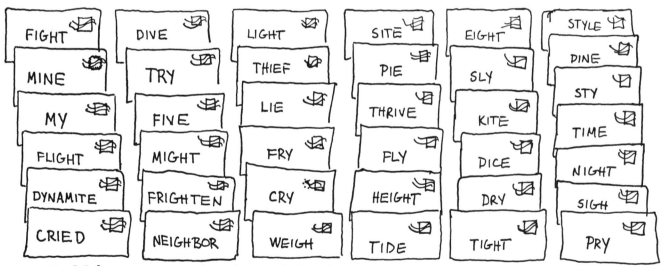

5. Make an answer key for each box by printing the words for each on separate pieces of paper. Glue the answer keys to the bottoms of the appropriate boxes.

6. Place all materials in a quiet corner of the classroom for students' free-time use.

PROCEDURE

1. Mail the envelopes by dropping them into the correct boxes.

2. After you complete the activity, check your work against the answer keys on the bottoms of the boxes.

FILL THE OUCH BASKET

PURPOSE: Practice in recognizing and
identifying "ou" words

PREPARATION

1. Gather the following materials.
   —brown and pastel shades of construction paper
   —felt pens
   —scissors
   —box with top

2. Use the egg pattern on the next page to draw as many eggs as needed on the pastel-colored construction paper. Cut out the eggs, and print the following "ou" words (and others of your choice) on the eggs

"ou" Words

thousand	outer	count	mouse	doubt	hour
counter	round	bounce	ground	about	out
mountain	found	pound	mouth	south	bout

Other Words

journey	could	should	would	pour	four

3. Make a basket from the brown construction paper, using the pattern on the next page. Cut as many slits in the basket as needed to hold the "ou" words. On the back of the basket, print the list of correct "ou" words to make this a self-checking activity.

4. Place all materials in a flat box. Print the following directions on the box top and place in a learning center, or make the activity available for individual student use.

PROCEDURE

1. Fill the empty "Ouch" basket with "ou" eggs. Read each egg to yourself, and think carefully about the sound of the word. If the word has the sound of "ou" as in "Ouch," place the egg in a slit in the basket.

2. After you have completed the activity, check your work against the list on the back of the basket.

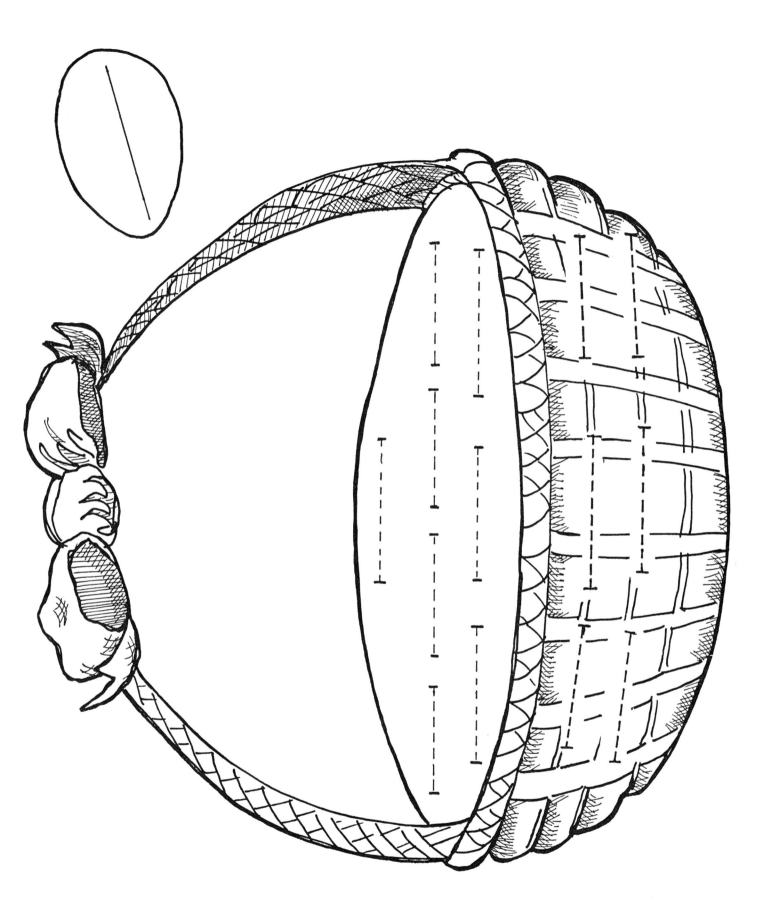

Fill the "ouch" Basket

SEEK AND FIND VOWEL SOUNDS

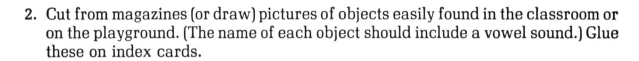

PURPOSE: Using vowel sounds

PREPARATION

    1. Gather the following materials.
        —3″ x 5″ index cards
        —pencils
        —magazines
        —scissors

    2. Cut from magazines (or draw) pictures of objects easily found in the classroom or on the playground. (The name of each object should include a vowel sound.) Glue these on index cards.

    3. Provide extra blank index cards and pencils.

        Note: This is not a game to play with the whole class or with a large group of students. It is ideal for small reading groups or for two or three children who need extra reinforcement. About ten minutes will be good timing for most groups.

PROCEDURE

    1. Select four or five cards from the stack, and try to locate the objects in the assigned time period.

    2. As each object is located, write the name of it on the index card provided. Underline the vowel sound, and beside the word, tell if it is a long or short vowel.

    3. Continue until all objects are located and recorded.

    4. The student who finishes first or who locates the most objects before "time" is called wins the game.

WORD MAKEOVER

PURPOSE: Using initial consonants

PREPARATION

1. Prepare tagboard word squares and consonant letter strips as shown on this page.

2. Provide pencils and paper for student use, and place all materials in a convenient spot for students to use as a free time activity.

PROCEDURE

1. Choose a letter strip and a square. Pull the strip through the opening in the square to make words by combining the initial consonants with the other letters. Write your words on a sheet of paper.

BOHEMIAN BLENDS

PURPOSE: Recognizing and using initial consonant blends

PREPARATION

1. Provide a very large sheet of paper and felt pens for students' use.

2. Use a sheet of the paper to start a free-form scribble drawing with a word beginning with one initial consonant blend.

3. Place the paper and a variety of felt pens in an accessible place in the classroom.

4. Use different blends over a period of time. Exhibit completed drawings together, or tape them together to form one giant mural.

PROCEDURE

1. Add words beginning with the same consonant blend to the drawing during the day.

2. Use different colors and different styles of writing to add interest to the drawing.

22

THE GREAT CONSONANT CASE

Fill in the missing consonants.

I__ you wor__ care__ully, you ca__ __ind the missin__ consonan__s ri__ht un__er Sly Sam t__e Sleut__'s eyes. Cir__le a co__sonant whe__ you __ut it in its p__oper pla__e, and you will __now __ot to go loo__ing __or it a__ain.

__ly Sa__ ha__ bee__ a__si__ne__ __o the __reat Co__sonan__ Ca__e. __on__onants __eep __isappea__ing i__ lar__e num__ers ri__ht ou__ o__ othe__wi__e sensi__le sen__ence__. More consonants a__e mis__ing eve__y __ay. The wor__s a__e be__inning to __anic, and

thou__h Sly Sam i__ smar__ and __rave, eve__ he is despe-rate. Ca__ you co__e to his re__cue?

Please hu__ __y and repla__e the missing consonants to re__urn peace and __uiet to Sly Sam's worl__.

The one stray vowel and five leftover consonants bring a message to you from Sly Sam. Write the message here.

"_____!!"

23

SILENT SKYSCRAPER

PURPOSE: Practice in recognizing silent consonants

PREPARATION
1. Provide copies of the "Silent Skyscraper" work sheet on the following page and pencils for each participant.

PROCEDURE
1. Begin at #1 and silently pronounce the word. If the word contains a silent consonant, find the next word in numerical order with a silent consonant, and draw a line between the two. (If the **very** next word does not contain a silent consonant, that word is skipped. Go on to the next word.)

2. Continue to "test" words silently, and draw lines connecting the words with silent consonants until the complete outline appears.

3. If a "break" appears in the outline, you have missed a silent consonant word. Go back and check your work.

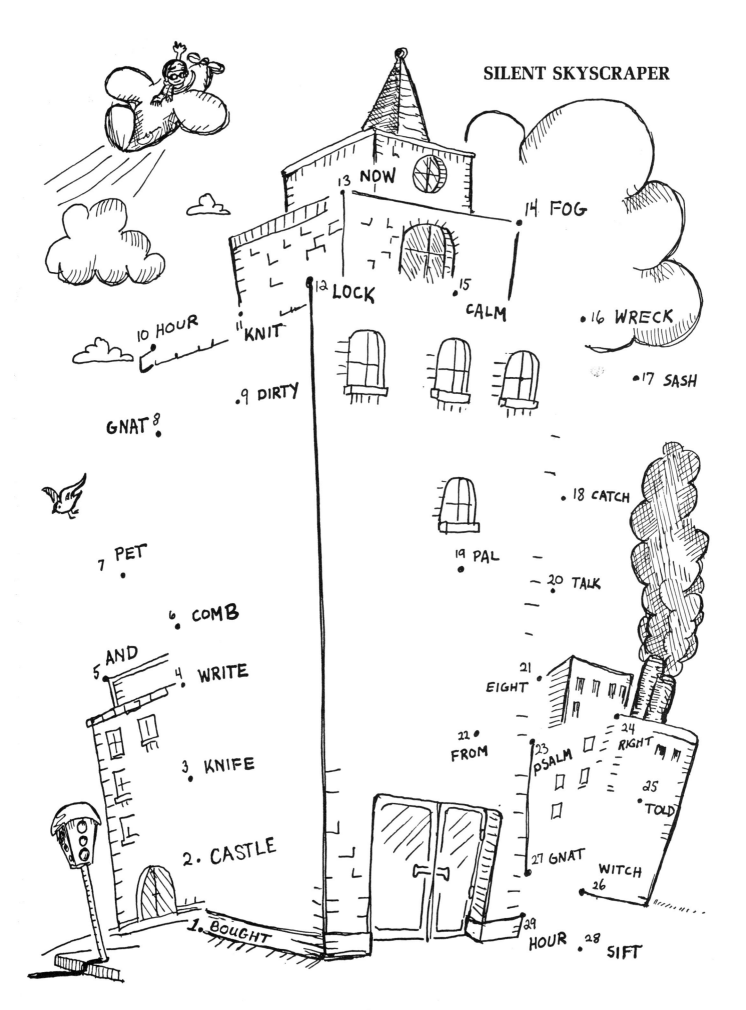

SILENT SKYSCRAPER

25

IS IT "D" OR "T"?

When **-ed** is added to the end of a word but does not form another syllable, the **-ed** sounds like **D** or **T**. Read each word below. Write the words with **D** ending sounds in the big D and the words with **T** ending sounds in the big T.

LOOKED   WALKED   CALLED   ROLLED   MARCHED
SMOKED   CHARGED   BUMPED   PLANTED   SLASHED
SHOCKED   ALLOWED   STACKED   TRACKED   FOLLOWED

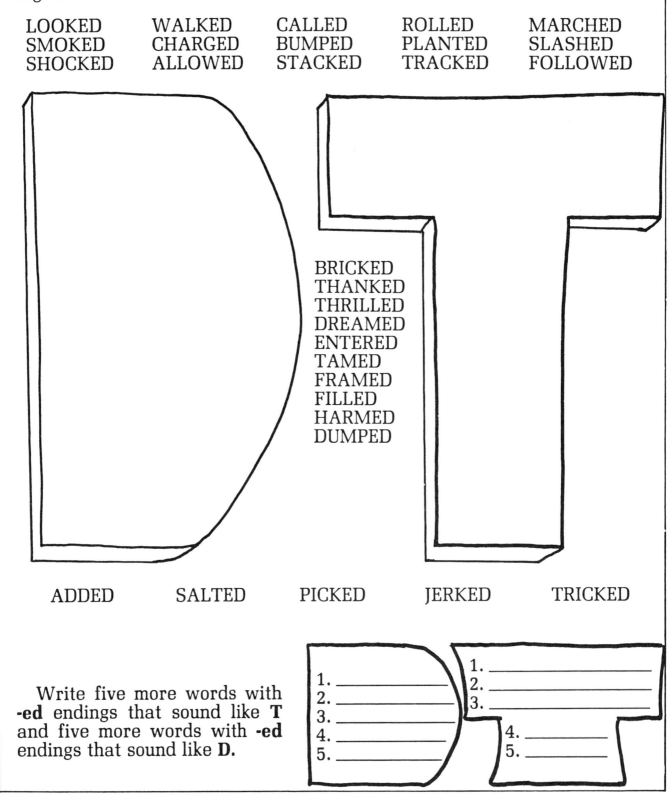

BRICKED
THANKED
THRILLED
DREAMED
ENTERED
TAMED
FRAMED
FILLED
HARMED
DUMPED

ADDED   SALTED   PICKED   JERKED   TRICKED

Write five more words with **-ed** endings that sound like **T** and five more words with **-ed** endings that sound like **D**.

1. _____
2. _____
3. _____
4. _____
5. _____

1. _____
2. _____
3. _____
4. _____
5. _____

LETTER-ING

Read the words below and decide if the last letter should be doubled or dropped before -ing is added to the word. Write each word with the -ing ending in the correct "Letter-ing" box.

hop	plan	time	sit	live	hope
come	wake	tap	swim	love	bat
grin	shore	strike	fan	trim	like

DOUBLED LETTER-ING

DROPPED LETTER-ING

LOOK ALIKES

PURPOSE: Final sound discrimination/word association

PREPARATION
1. Make copies of the work sheet on the following page, and give one to each student.

PROCEDURE
A. Final sound discrimination
   1. The teacher chooses one word from each block and reads it aloud.

   2. Students listen as the teacher reads, and draw circles around the words pronounced.

B. Word Association
   1. The student crosses out the word that does not belong.

   2. The student draws a star around the plural form of each word.

LOOK ALIKES

NAME _Jennifer_   DATE _Caplener_

1	PENCILS	PENNY	PENCIL
2	PAN	PAT	PANS
3	TOE	TOES	TOP
4	HATS	HOT	HAT
5	TREE	SEE	TREES
6	STOP	STOPS	STRIP
7	COW	COT	COWS
8	BALL	BELLS	BELL
9	BUG	BAG	BUGS
10	ROCKS	RACK	ROCK
11	STRAPS	STRIP	STRAP
12	STRING	BRING	STRINGS

TWENTY-FIVE POINTS

PURPOSE: Making words by combining beginning consonant blends with word endings

PREPARATION

1. Provide the following materials.
   —game board
   —3″ x 5″ cards
   —markers
   —spinner
   —pencils and paper for scorekeeping

2. Reproduce the game board.

3. Write ending sounds on cards.

4. Provide a marker for each player.

5. Place the game in a learning center or in a free-time activity center.

PROCEDURE

1. This game is for three or more players.

2. Place the cards face down on the game board.

3. The first player spins, moves that number of spaces and draws a card. Using the ending on the card and beginning sound in the square landed on, the player makes as many words as possible. Extra letters or syllables may be added in the middle so long as the beginning and ending sounds are kept in place.

   Example: Beginning sound—bl   Ending Sound—ed

   Words Formed
   —bled
   —blinked
   —blurted
   —blunted
   —bloated

   A player's score for each turn equals the number of words made during that turn.

4. Players continue to take turns until one reaches twenty-five points and wins the game.

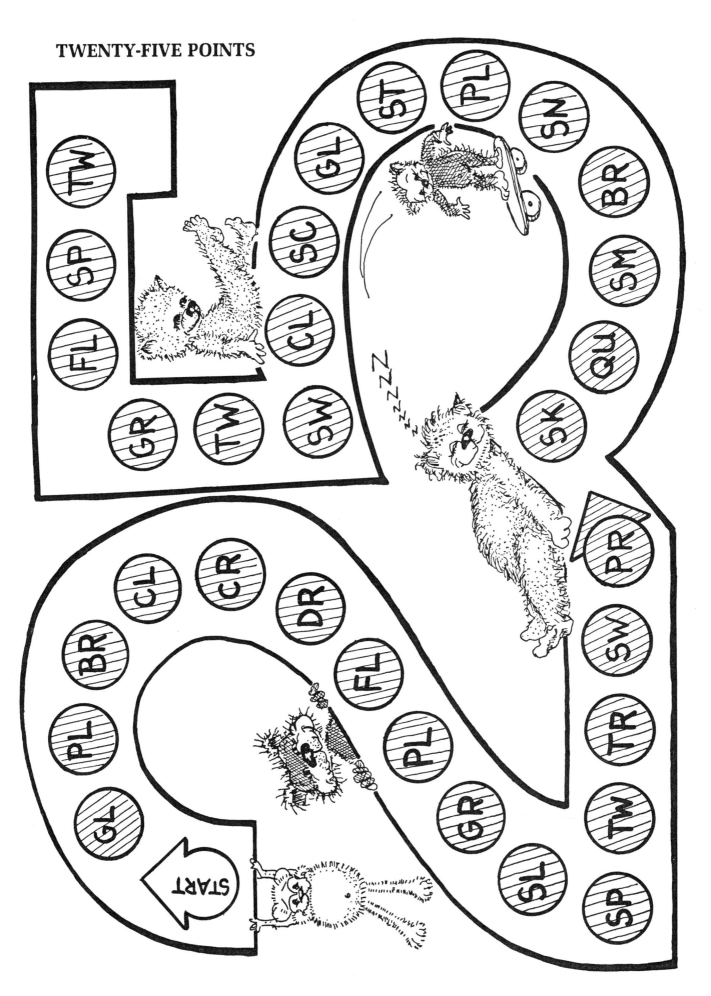

UNDER THE PHONICS UMBRELLA

Color all the consonant spaces yellow. Color all the vowel spaces orange. Color the rest of the picture as you like.

Circle all the long "u" sounds in the following sentence.

Ursula Upchurch waited under the umbrella until her uncle

had unpacked his unused ukuleke.

PHONICS FOOLERS

A "Phonics Fooler" is a joke or rhyme written in phonetic notation. Translate this fooler by writing its English version on the lines beside it.

Yo͞o dōn't nēd ā ro͞o'-lər
To͞o trăns-lāt' this fo͞o'-lər
Jŭst yo͞oz ôl yo͞o nō
ə-bout' fŏn'-ĭks, ənd GŌ!

_____
_____
_____
_____

Make up 6 "Phonics Foolers" of your own, and write them in the spaces below. Find the correct phonetic form for each word in a dictionary. Exchange papers with a classmate, and rewrite his/her foolers in English. Then discuss your translations.

33

CIRCLE AROUND

PURPOSE: Using rhyming words

PREPARATION
1. Gather the following materials.
    —black or red construction paper
    —magazine pictures
    —scissors
    —tagboard
    —paste
    —coffee can and top

2. Cut out several small circles from tagboard, and paste magazine pictures on them.

3. Cut out larger circles from black or red construction paper. Make a slit in each circle so that the tagboard circles can be inserted into them.

4. Place all the materials in a decorated coffee can, and print the title on the outside.

PROCEDURE
1. Choose a tagboard circle picture.

2. Insert it into the construction paper slit.

3. Name as many words that rhyme with the picture as possible.

SUPER SHAPE-UP

PURPOSE: Recognizing and using rhyming words

PREPARATION

1. Glue the two halves of the "Super Shape-Up" game board inside a file folder.

2. Reproduce the "Super Shape-Up" rhyming word sheets.

3. Cut the shapes apart, and place them in an envelope.

4. On the outside of the envelope, print the directions given below.

5. Place the folder and the envelope in an accessible place for individual student use.

PROCEDURE

1. Match the rhyming pictures, and place them on the correct shapes.

2. Pronounce the words.

ADAPTATIONS

This game could be adapted to teach word association by using words in the squares, or to teach upper and lower case letter recognition by putting letters in the squares.

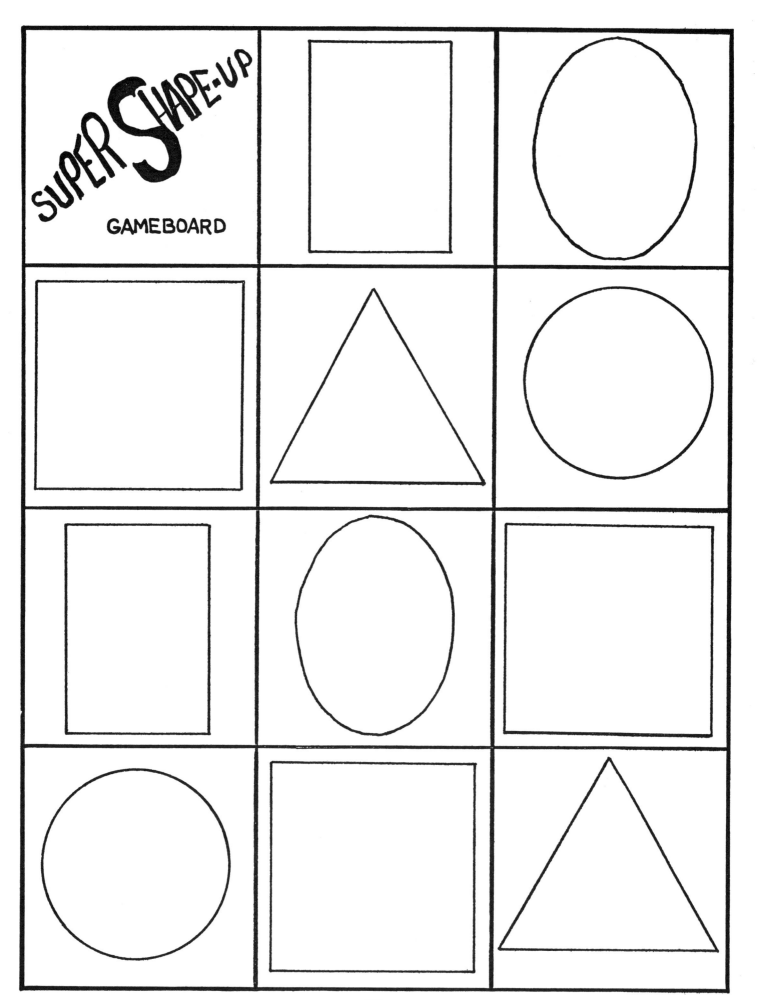

SUPER SHAPE-UP
GAMEBOARD

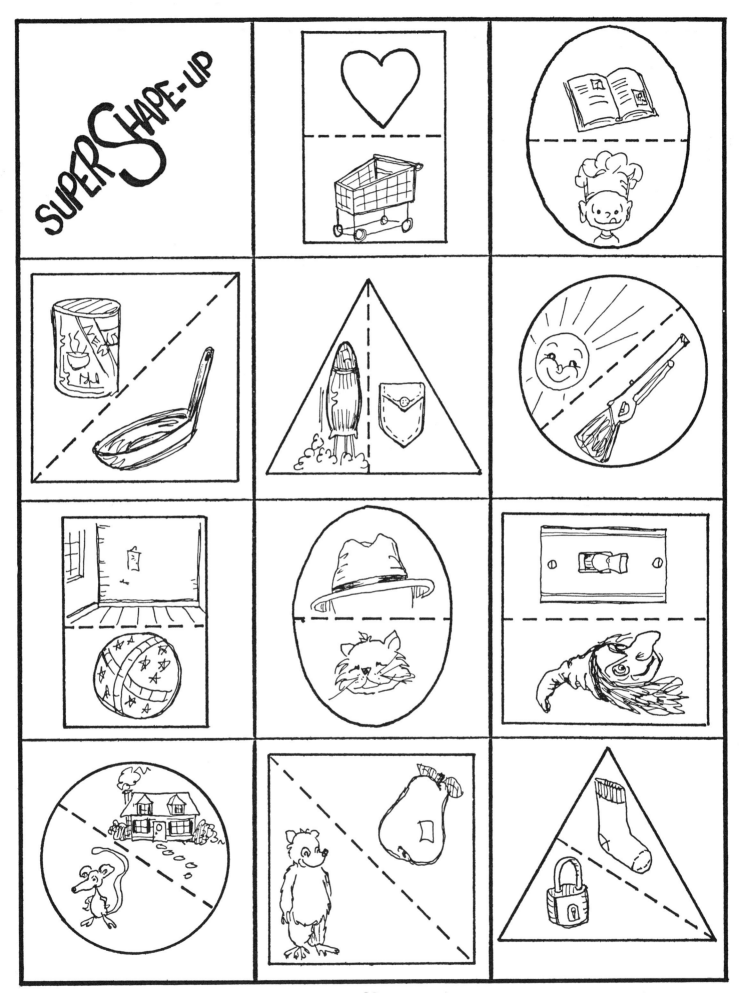

SUPER SHAPE-UP

SYLLABLE SAIL

PURPOSE: Identifying and using syllables

PREPARATION

1. Enlarge the "Syllable Sail" gameboard.

2. Cut sailboat markers from construction paper.

3. Make word cards with the following or other ocean-related words.

sailing	aquanaut	sponges	underwater
ocean	coral	algae	depth
vessel	snorkel	fathom	stern
waves	plankton	whale	aqualung
porpoise	scuba	ship	lighthouse
mollusks	ahoy	bow	regatta
port	starboard	boat	swimmers
divers	deck	sea	oceanography

PROCEDURE

1. This game is for two or more players.

2. Place the stack of word cards in the center of the board.

3. Each player selects a sailboat marker and places it on the board.

4. Players take turns drawing a card and moving one space forward for each syllable in the word. If the number of syllables is incorrectly guessed, the player moves **back** that same number of syllables.

5. The first player to reach "Home Port" wins the game.

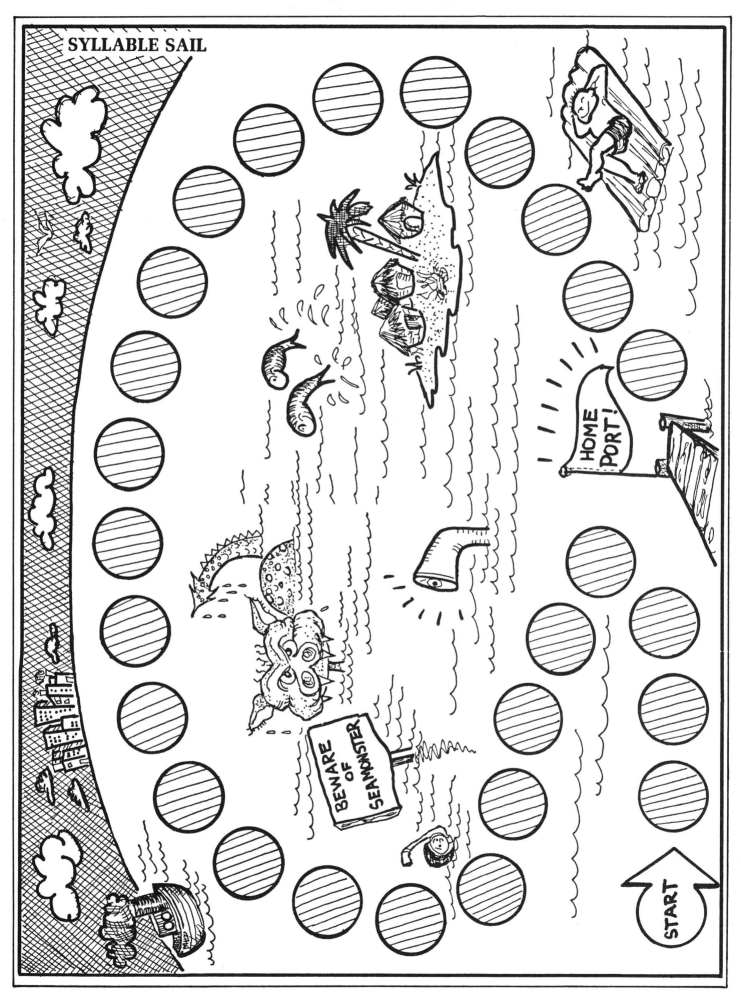

SPEAKING IN SYLLABLES

PURPOSE: Recognizing and using syllables

PREPARATION
1. Provide the following materials for the students.
   —"Speaking in Syllables" game board
   —markers
   —die

2. Reproduce the "Speaking in Syllables" game board. Write other words of one, two and three syllables in the squares if the ones shown are not appropriate.

3. Provide one die and a marker for each student.

PROCEDURE
1. This game is for two or more players.

2. The first player throws the die and moves the marker that number of spaces. If the square landed on contains a one-syllable word, the player pronounces the word correctly and moves forward one space. If the marker lands on a space containing a two-syllable word, the player pronounces the word and moves forward two spaces. If the player lands on a three-syllable word space and pronounces the word correctly, he/she receives another turn. (If the player mispronounces the word, the extra move is forfeited.)

3. The other players continue the game in the same manner. The first player to go around the board three times wins.

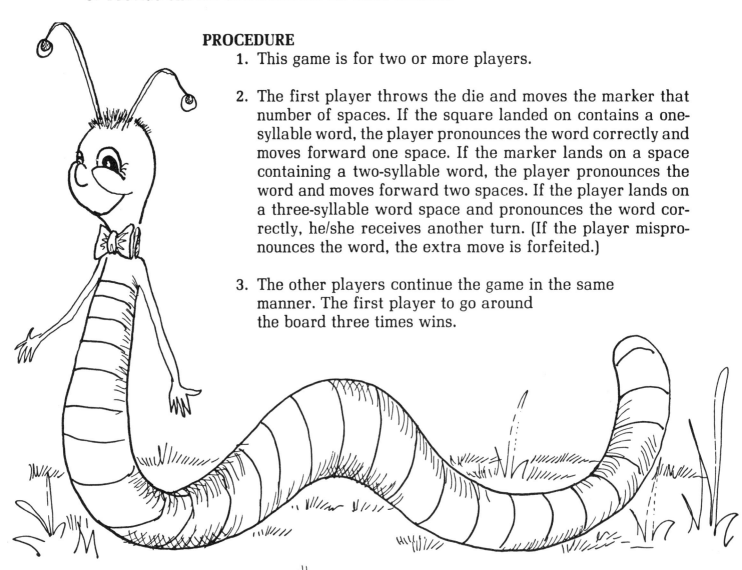

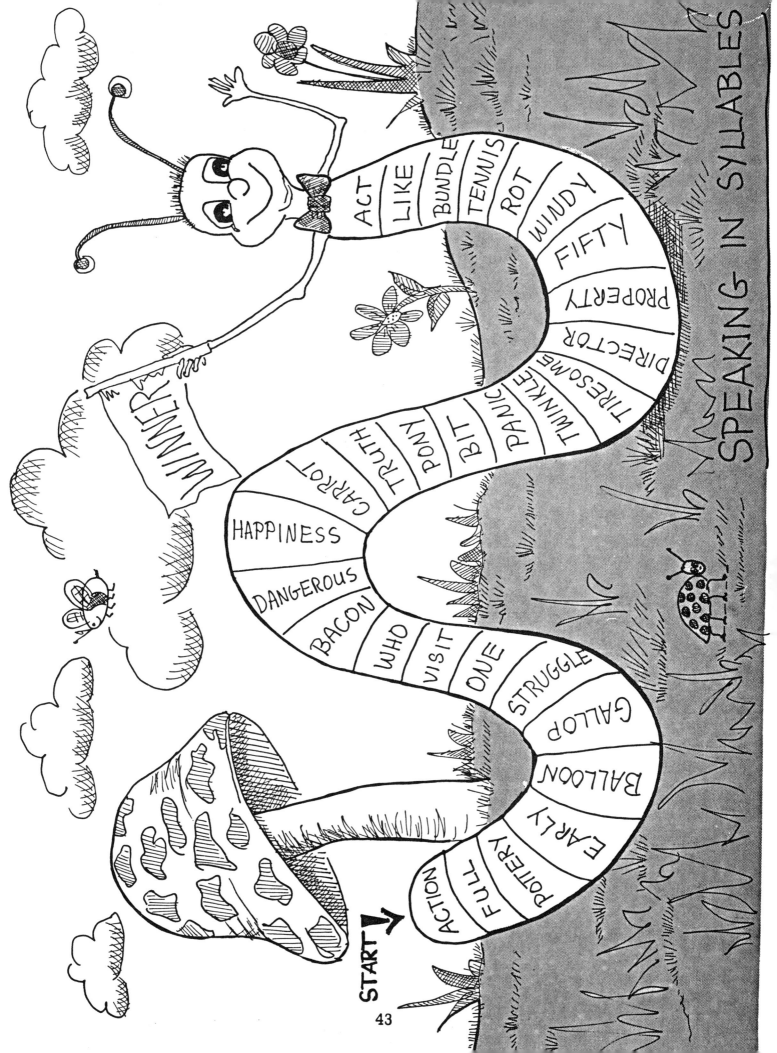

PURPOSE: Using accent marks

PREPARATION

1. Use brightly colored felt pens to line sheets of writing paper vertically to make three columns.

2. Print two- and three-syllable words on 3" x 5" cards or on strips of construction paper.

3. Place the words in a box or basket, and pass it around for each student to select twenty. (Adjust the number of the cards to the maturity level of the students.)

4. Provide scissors, paste, pencils and the Procedure directions for the students.

PROCEDURE

1. Read each of your words carefully.

2. Cut each word apart into syllables.

3. Paste one syllable in each column.

4. Place the accent marks in the correct places.

5. Write your full name on the bottom of the paper. Divide it into syllables, and place the accent marks correctly.

EXTEND - A - WORD

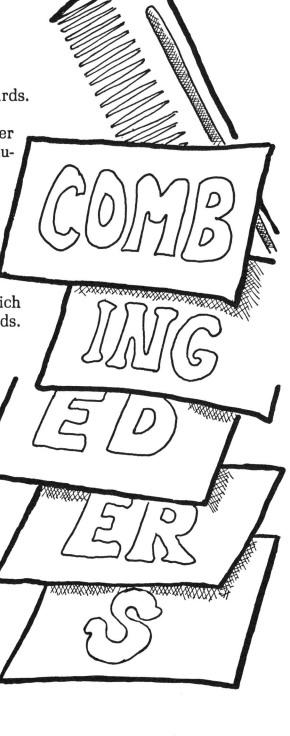

PURPOSE: Adding endings to root words

PREPARATION

1. Gather the following materials.
   - —3″ x 5″ cards
   - —felt pen
   - —paper
   - —pencils

2. Write root words on 3″ x 5″ cards.

3. Write word endings on separate 3″ x 5″ cards.

4. Place the two stacks of cards in a quiet corner along with writing paper and pencils for student use.

PROCEDURE

1. This activity is for an individual student.

2. Choose one root word card.

3. Find as many word endings as possible which can be added to that word to make new words.

4. Write the word at the top of a sheet of paper, and list the new words made under it.

45

PURPOSE: Using prefixes

PREPARATION

1. Gather the following materials.
   —wooden clothespins
   (spring-type)
   —construction paper
   —clothesline
   —felt pen

2. Print prefixes on clothespins. If plastic ones are used, print prefixes on strips of paper and glue to pins.

3. Make construction paper clothes (see patterns), and print a root word on each one.

4. String a clothesline across one corner of the classroom or along the chalkboard ledge.

PROCEDURE

1. Clip the root word clothes to the clothesline using a prefix clothespin that can be combined with the root word to make a new word.

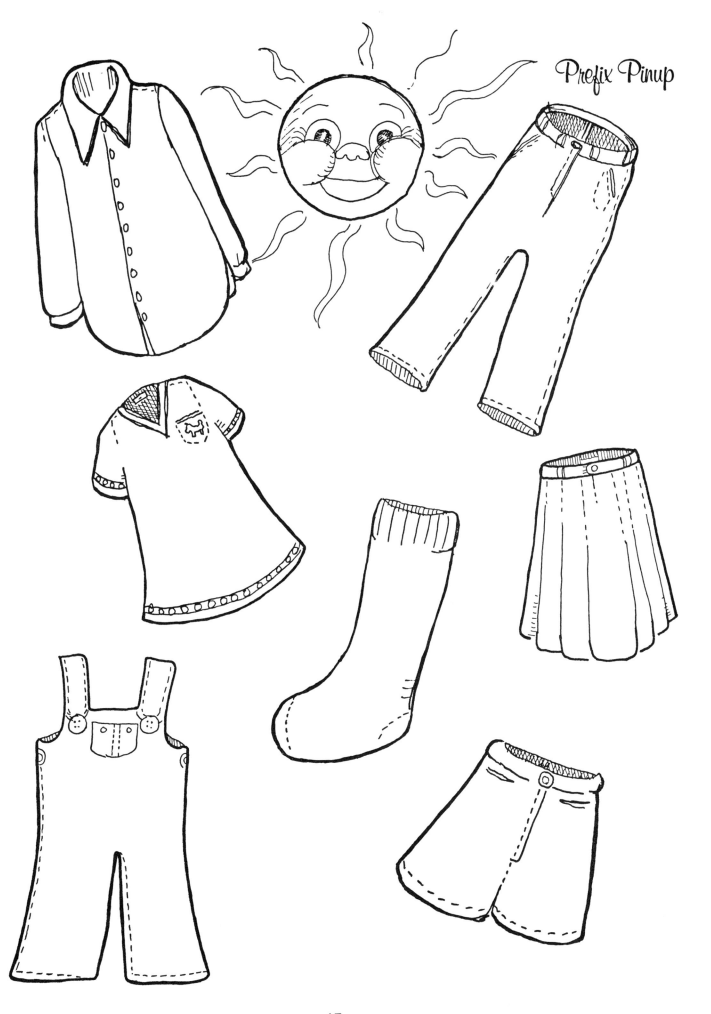

Prefix Pinup

47

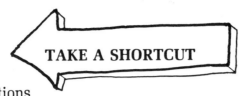

TAKE A SHORTCUT

PURPOSE: Using abbreviations

PREPARATION

1. Reproduce the story on the following page to be used as either an individual work sheet or as a learning center activity.

2. Provide pencils or pens for the students.

PROCEDURE

1. Read the story carefully the first time. Then reread it, circling all words in the story that could be abbreviated.

2. Match the circled words with the abbreviations at the bottom of the page.

3. Write each word beside its matching abbreviation.

A Tragic Tale

Mistress Evans, who lives in the Tower Apartment Building on Centennial Boulevard, fell down the stairs and broke her leg. Her neighbor, Mister Bradley, saw her fall, and immediately telephoned Doctor Tugwell at his office on West Main Street. Since it was Monday morning, September first, the office was closed as everyone was on holiday.

Thinking quickly, Mister Bradley dialed the number for Saint Andrews Hospital on Westchester Avenue, and asked for the Emergency Department. He explained the situation to a nurse who said, "Tell Mistress Evans that an ambulance from Hospital Helpers, Incorporated, is on the way now to pick her up and bring her here."

Mister Bradley hurried back to Mistress Evans with the good news. Mistress Evans was relieved to know that help was on the way, but she was very angry that she had fallen at all. She said, "It's all the building superintendent's fault! If he had fixed that broken step three weeks ago when we reported it, none of this would have happened. I'm going to call my attorney and sue!!!"

About that time, Captain Norton of Ships, International, came up the stairs. "Avast there, you lubbers," he boomed, "you look like a ship stuck on a sandbar! What's the problem?"

Mister Bradley told Captain Norton what had happened, and Mistress Evans repeated her plans to sue. The captain nodded his head sympathetically and said, "Tell your attorney to contact the Sunshine Realty Company at 29 South Watley Court. They own this building, and would be the responsible party."

Suddenly Mistress Evans exclaimed, "Hush! Do you hear a siren?" The two men strained their ears, but just as they decided that they had heard nothing, there was a noise at the bottom of the stairs. Three people in white uniforms carrying a six-foot long stretcher entered the stairwell and looked up. Captain Norton exclaimed, "Right this way . . . right up here! Hurry —we've been waiting for at least an hour, and this lady's leg has swollen up as big as a gallon jug! Look lively there! You've already wasted five minutes just staring! What you need is six months in the Navy. That will teach you to move!"

The ambulance people ran up the stairs, put Mistress Evans on the stretcher and bundled her into the ambulance. As they drove away, Mister Bradley shook his head and said, "Poor Mistress Evans. It's too bad that she had to start the Fall with a fall!"

Abbreviations

Ct. _____	supt. _____	Sept. _____	Mrs. _____
St. _____	1st _____	Bldg. _____	Dept. _____
ft. _____	min. _____	Blvd. _____	Capt. _____
mo. _____	Mon. _____	a.m. _____	Apt. _____
Mr. _____	wks. _____	Ave. _____	Dr. _____
W. _____	St. _____	Inc. _____	att. _____
Co. _____	hr. _____	gal. _____	S. _____

CONTRACTION FRACTIONS

 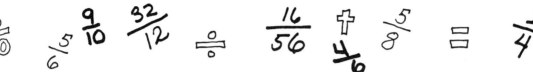

You know that when you work with fractions in math, you must reduce them to the lowest common denominator. Contractions are like fractions because they "reduce" 2 words into 1 smaller word. Work the "Contraction Fractions" below.

$\dfrac{do}{not}$ = _____ $\dfrac{I}{am}$ = _____ $\dfrac{we}{are}$ = _____

$\dfrac{he}{is}$ = _____ $\dfrac{should}{not}$ = _____ $\dfrac{you}{have}$ = _____

$\dfrac{would}{not}$ = _____ $\dfrac{it}{is}$ = _____ $\dfrac{they}{are}$ = _____

$\dfrac{she}{will}$ = _____ $\dfrac{are}{not}$ = _____ $\dfrac{there}{is}$ = _____

$\dfrac{was}{not}$ = _____ $\dfrac{you}{will}$ = _____ $\dfrac{can}{not}$ = _____

$\dfrac{you}{are}$ = _____ $\dfrac{will}{not}$ = _____ $\dfrac{has}{not}$ = _____

$\dfrac{were}{not}$ = _____ $\dfrac{I}{will}$ = _____ $\dfrac{does}{not}$ = _____

Put the answers to your "Contraction Fractions" into action by writing a short story titled "Mr. Jackson's Reaction." Include at least 10 contractions, and underline each in the color of your choice.

WORD SLIDE

The words below are compound words, and have special meanings because they are "add-on" words. Circle one part of each word to "slide" off. Draw a picture to show the entirely different meaning of the remaining word.

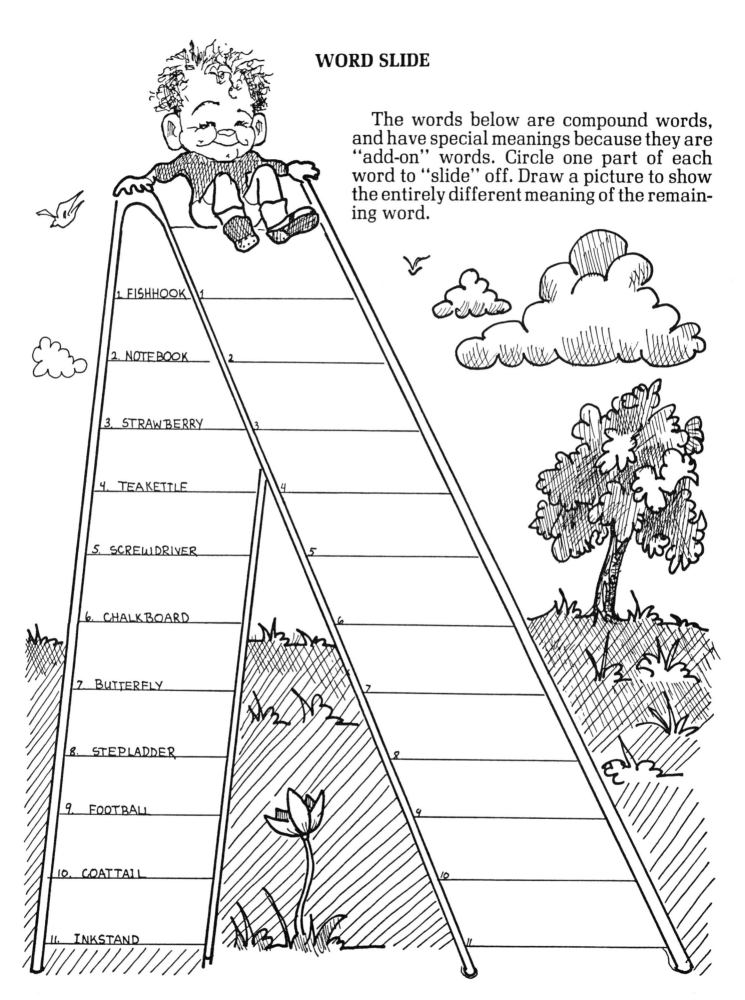

1. FISHHOOK   1
2. NOTEBOOK   2
3. STRAWBERRY   3
4. TEAKETTLE   4
5. SCREWDRIVER   5
6. CHALKBOARD   6
7. BUTTERFLY   7
8. STEPLADDER   8
9. FOOTBALL   9
10. COATTAIL   10
11. INKSTAND   11

COMPOUND CANVAS

PURPOSE: Practice in recognizing compound words

PREPARATION

    1. Reproduce a copy of the word-find puzzle on the next page for each participant, and provide pencils or pens for each.

PROCEDURE

    1. Circle all compound words with a pencil or pen. The words are listed horizontally, vertically, diagonally, forward and backward.

    2. The first participant to find all fifty-three words is the winner.

COMPOUND CANVAS

```
G B R O O M S T I C K N A T I O S D N E R
R C A R D B O A R D A Y L D S T I N N V E
E A A S S A T E D R A Y N R A B D A A E P
E M R N K S T R A W B E R R Y O L L M R A
N P Y O Y E H E Y L E C F R O P O M K Y P
H F A W A B T N P C T I E W R Y E R L O S
O I D M W A A B A R S W E I C A O A I N W
U R H A E L M L A H O R A P L W C F M E E
S E T N V L P C E L I T C E A H S X R G N
E E R N I E G A F F L R H A N G O D O I O
E M I T R E T N I W P L A Y T I M E A B E
R I B I D S U N N A E M I E N H E T D U M
E T F P O S T O R T S P R G U W D B S L O
H E I P A O B T R E C S M N H A A E I O S
T M S N O O E E D R H O A E Y T Y D D N E
O O H O D S K T M F O M N D I E H R E N M
M S E Y U A T A A A O E O V E R C O A T I
D T R O C I O M N L L B A L S M U O U R T
N P M N R I S Y A L Y O E H A E P M P S D
A Y A H O L I A D N A D D O L L H O U S E
R P N A M S E L A S R Y E S U O H D R I B
G R O W N U P P O R D N I A R N H A Y S T
```

53

COMPOUND COUNTDOWN

PURPOSE: Recognizing and using
          compound words

PREPARATION
1. Gather the following materials.
   —clock or timer
   —5″ x 7″ index cards
   —felt pen
   —paper and pencils
   —box

2. Print 20 to 40 words on index cards. Use these or other words.

ball	coat	sail	book	boy	shore	school
brush	place	bone	rain	pan	room	sun
pop	bath	eye	dog	tub	tooth	snow
house	fire	one	man	ship	plane	basket
dish	corn	rail	time	camp	shine	class

3. Place the word cards along with a timer (or clock) and pencils and paper in the box.

PROCEDURE
1. This game is for two players, or may be used as an individual activity.

2. Cards are turned face down in a stack.

3. At the beginning signal, each player draws a card, reads the word on it and writes the word on a piece of paper. The player thinks of as many compound words as possible that he/she can make using that word, and lists the compound words under the word.

4. When the timer signals "Time's up," each player draws another card, writes the word on his/her paper and continues in the same manner.

5. After fifteen words have been drawn and listed, the player with more compound words on his/her paper wins the game.

COMPOUND MUSEUM

Fill the museum walls with original compound word portraits. The first one is done for you — you do the rest.

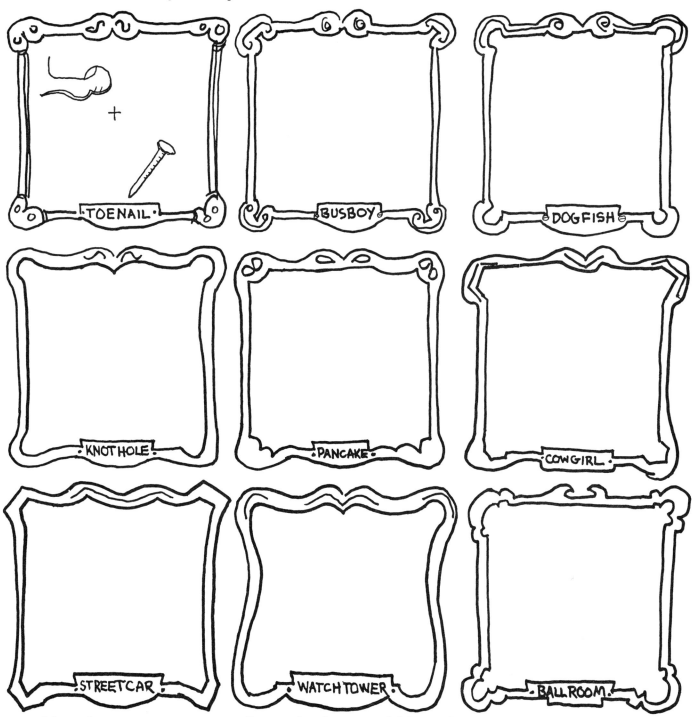

List nine more compound words that could be added to the museum collection.

1. _____   2. _____   3. _____
4. _____   5. _____   6. _____
7. _____   8. _____   9. _____

PLURAL DECISIONS

To solve the puzzle and find the hidden word, mark T (for True) or F (for False) beside each sentence below. If the sentence is true, color the puzzle spaces indicated. (For example, if sentence #1 is true, color all of the #1 spaces in the puzzle.)

__ 1. To make the word **baby** mean more than one, change the **y** to **i** and add **es**.

__ 2. To make the word **fox** mean more than one, add **es**.

__ 3. To make the word **boy** mean more than one, change the **y** to **i** and add **es**.

__ 4. To make the word **knife** mean more than one, change the **fe** to **v** and add **es**.

__ 5. To make the word **girl** mean more than one, add **es**.

__ 6. To make the word **clock** mean more than one, change the **k** to **i** and add **es**.

__ 7. To make the word **flower** mean more than one, add **s**.

__ 8. To make the word **church** mean more than one, add **s**.

__ 9. To make the word **pencil** mean more than one, add **s**.

Now, write the plural form of each of the following words:

monkey   bird   party   porch   tax   noun   life

POSITIVELY POSSESSIVES

Read the following sentences. If a sentence has a word containing an apostrophe to show **possession**, color in the spaces in the picture that have that sentence number. (Example: if sentence #1 contains a word with an apostrophe to show possession, color in the #1 spaces.)

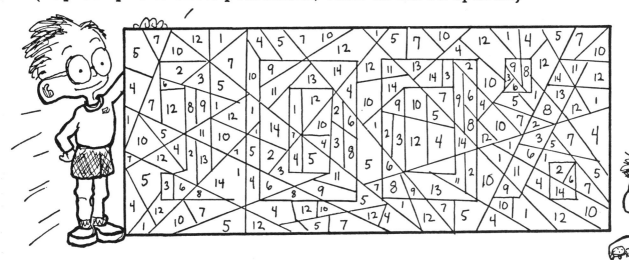

1. Matthew's day started off badly.

2. First, he couldn't find his shoes.

3. Then he remembered that he didn't do his homework.

4. His mother's car was broken, so he had to walk to school.

5. When he finally got to class, his teacher's question was, "Why are you so late?'

6. Matthew answered sadly, "I'm sorry, but everything just went wrong this morning."

7. Matthew started to do his classwork, but his pencil's point broke.

8. "I can't stand this much longer," thought Matthew.

9. "Never mind," whispered his friend April, "here's another one for you."

10. When test time came, Matthew's teacher handed out the papers.

11. Matthew groaned, "I'll never be able to answer all these questions!"

12. When he finished, he handed in his paper and watched the teacher's red pen move across his page.

13. "Good for you, Matthew," said his teacher at last, "you've made 100%!"

14. Matthew grinned and said, "Wow! Hasn't this day improved!"

Choose a Cloud

WEAR / WERE

RARE / REAR

WITCH / WHICH

THEIR / THERE

DARE / DEAR

RING / RANG

FLIT / FLAT

SUN / SUM

COULD / CLOUD

Read the sentence sets below and decide which cloud word pair goes with each. Write those words in the cloud beside each set. Then complete the sentences by writing in the correct word from the word pair selected.

I'd like to _____ the blue dress.
Where _____ you when I needed you?

This ground is as _____ as my hand.
Fireflies _____ to and fro at dusk.

She ordered her roast beef _____.
That _____ door needs fixing.

The desert _____ is unbelievably hot.
Adding two numbers together will give you the _____.

People go _____ to shop.
_____ dog disappeared.

The Halloween _____ looked scary.
_____ of these bikes do you like best?

_____ I go with you?
The dark _____ moved across the sky.

The telephone bell _____ loudly.
I heard the six o'clock bell _____.

Books are especially _____ to the librarian.
I _____ you to tell that story again.

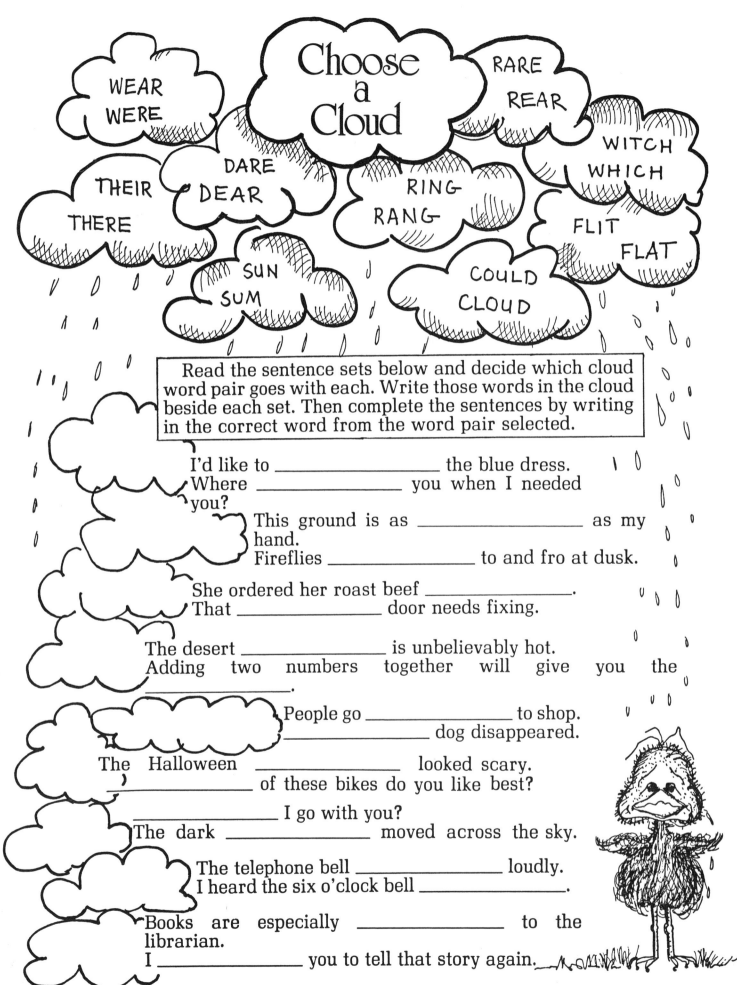

58

WORD RECOGNITION SKILLS COMPETENCY REVIEW

1. Draw a line from each word to the sound the vowel makes.

   cry   ie
   kite   y
   frighten   igh

2. Draw a line from each word ending to the initial consonant with which it can be combined to make a word.

   ue   k
   ot   l
   it   q

3. Draw a circle around the word which has a silent consonant sound.

   dirty
   knife
   told

4. Draw a circle around the word beginning with a consonant blend.

   mark
   play
   ten

5. Draw a circle around the word which ends in -**ed** and sounds like **D** rather than **T**.

   jerked
   added
   dumped

6. Draw a line from each beginning consonant blend to the word ending with which it can be combined to form a word.

   bl   ip
   dr   oat
   pl   ant

7. Draw a circle around the word in which the last letter should be dropped before -**ing** is added.

   cut
   come
   open

8. Draw a circle around the word in which the last letter should be doubled before -**ing** is added.

   strike
   hop
   hope

9. Draw a circle around the word which does not rhyme with the other two.

   cap
   tape
   tap

10. Draw a circle around the word which contains a long **u** sound.

    until
    queen
    used

11. Draw a circle around the word which contains two syllables and has the correct accent marks.

    cot'-ton
    moth-er'
    stu-dent'

12. Draw a circle around the word which is correctly divided into syllables.

    geo-graph-y
    veg-e-ta-ble
    cale-ndar

13. Put a check beside the set of letters that is a prefix.

> pose-
> thr-
> pre-

14. Put a check beside the set of letters that is a suffix.

> -tern
> -able
> -low

15. Draw a circle around the word that includes a suffix.

> sister
> excitement
> demand

16. Draw a circle around the word which includes a prefix.

> international
> morning
> frequent

17. Draw a line from the root word to the ending that will make it into a new word.

> hair   -ing
> kick   -are
> toaster   -te

18. Draw a line from each word to its abbreviation.

> Mister   Mrs.
> Monday   Mr.
> Mistress   Mon.

19. Draw a line under the word that is a compound word.

> helpless
> campground
> present

20. Draw a circle around the one phrase that contains a contraction.

> . . . my teacher's pencil . . .
> . . . the Green's house . . .
> . . . he doesn't care . . .

21. Draw a line under the one word that fits correctly into this sentence.

> The students looked _____ the windows at the rain.

> through
> thought
> trough

Word Usage Skills

II. WORD USAGE SKILLS

WORD MEANING

____Can use sight vocabulary

____Can use picture clues

____Can use context clues

____Can define words by classification or function

____Can understand multiple meanings of a given word

____Recognizes and can use common synonyms, antonyms and homonyms for familiar words

____Recognizes and can use key words in content areas

____Can interpret and convey meanings of a variety of familiar words.

WORD SENSITIVITY

____Can associate words with feelings

____Can form sensory impressions

____Can interpret figurative and idiomatic expressions

____Can interpret sensations and moods suggested by words

____Can recognize word relationships

____Can recognize and use descriptive words

____Is developing word appreciation

PRIVATE COLLECTION

PURPOSE: Developing sight word vocabulary

PREPARATION

1. Cut 3″ x 5″ index cards in half, or make cards from heavy scrap paper (colored paper is fun when available).

2. Print one word on each card to make flash cards. Use words of current importance to students (new words from reading texts, helping words, math or social studies words, names of countries, etc.).

3. As sets of cards are made, make "Collection Cards" for each group. Print each word in the group on one side of the cards. On the other, draw a line for the child's name and for the date of the award. Attach a gold star, a smiling face sticker, a symbol that means "success" and/or write or draw a message of your own. (Different messages may be used for each set of cards to add interest.)

PROCEDURE

1. Students use cards as flash cards, working in pairs, in small groups or individually.

2. When a student feels he/she can name all the words on sight, he/she asks for a "time with the teacher."

3. If all the words are identified correctly, the students is awarded a "Collection Card."

4. The object of this activity is to see who can build the largest card collection.

VOCABULARY VAULT

PURPOSE: Using sight vocabulary

PREPARATION
1. Gather the following materials.
   —oak tag
   —scissors
   —dictionaries
   —colored felt pens or crayons

2. Direct each child to bring an empty shoe box with a top to class.

3. Cut the oak tag into cards that will fit into the boxes.

4. Distribute a stack of blank cards to each student.

PROCEDURE
1. Students use the colored pens and/or crayons to decorate their boxes, and store the blank cards inside.

2. When a student needs to know the correct spelling or meaning of a word, he/she writes the word on a card and looks it up in the dictionary. The student writes the information found on the card, learns the information and files the card in the box for future reference.

3. A student may place any word he/she wishes to learn in the box. Words missed on spelling tests and unfamiliar words from content area texts and reference materials are good additions, too.

4. As the collections grow, students may use their cards as flash cards (two students share cards and check each other), for word games and in many other settings.

ADD-A-WORD

PURPOSE: Sight word vocabulary development

PREPARATION
1. Gather the following materials.
   —3″ x 5″ index cards
   —felt pen
   —pencils and paper
   —bell

2. Print each of the following and other words of your choice on index cards.

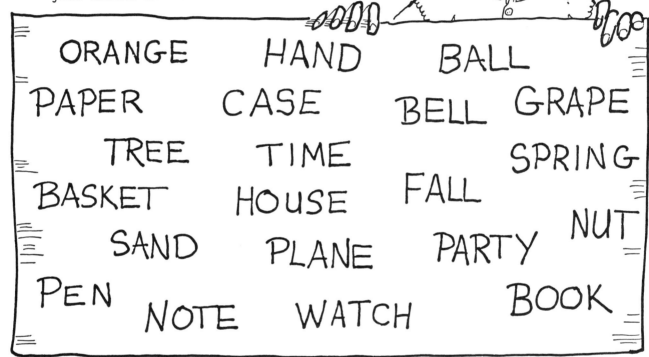

ORANGE   HAND   BALL
PAPER   CASE   BELL   GRAPE
TREE   TIME   SPRING
BASKET   HOUSE   FALL
SAND   PLANE   PARTY   NUT
PEN   NOTE   WATCH   BOOK

PROCEDURE
1. Players sit in a circle and pass the cards around, each player taking the top card from the stack. The cards are not looked at until the bell is rung.

2. At the sound of the bell, cards are turned over. Each player adds one word at a time to the word on the card to give it a new meaning, and repeats this process as many times as possible. No abbreviations and no apostrophies are allowed.

3. When the bell sounds again (time limit to be determined before the game begins), cards are passed to the left. Each player then begins a new list with the new word. The game continues in this manner.

4. When "time" is called, lists are compared. A winner is declared for each word, determined by the lengths of the lists.

REBUS RACE

Try your luck at reading these rebuses. Sit where you can see a clock. Time yourself to see how long it takes you to figure out each one. Write each message on the line below its rebus, and record your time in the box.

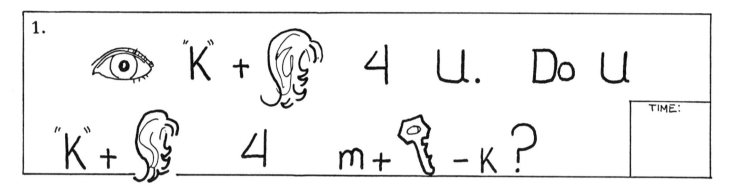

1. _____

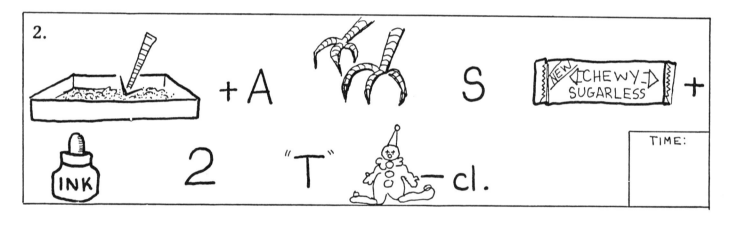

2. _____

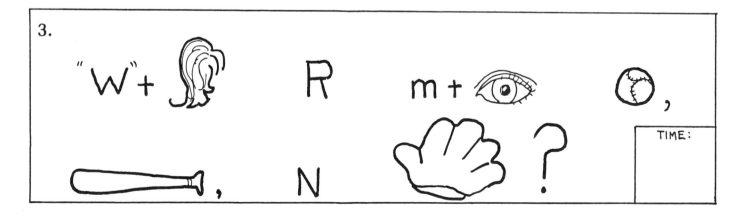

3. _____

REBUS RACE

4.

5.

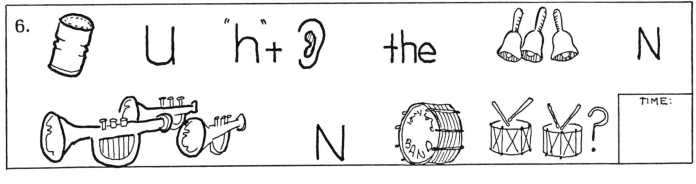

6.

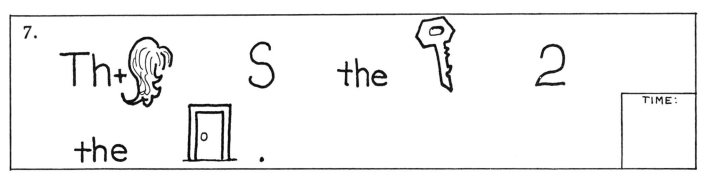

7.

IN CONTEXT

PURPOSE: Using context clues

PREPARATION

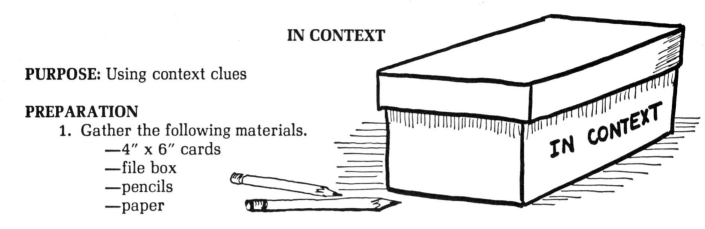

1. Gather the following materials.
   - —4″ x 6″ cards
   - —file box
   - —pencils
   - —paper

2. Make up several one-paragraph stories (or take simple short stories from basal texts or classroom newspapers). Eliminate all the adjectives, nouns or verbs from each story, and copy them over on 4″ x 6″ index cards, leaving blanks for the omitted words.

3. Reproduce the stories on the following page, and paste them on cards to be used as "starters" for your own collection.

4. Place the stories and the Procedure directions in a file box or shoe box.

PROCEDURE

1. Work in pairs to select two stories to copy over and fill in the blanks. Use one card at a time, and then exchange it with your partner.

2. When both stories are completed, exchange them with each other, and compare and contrast the turns your stories have taken.

It was a tense and exciting time at the Space Program Headquarters. The tremendous manned spacecraft was parked at its huge metal hangar, waiting for its well-trained passenger to board. The rocket engineers carefully checked every single electrical component to make sure that all systems were "GO," and the computer experts quickly fed the final technical and mathematical information into the main computer to make certain that nothing would go wrong. A tall dark man wearing a special green space suit and helmet appeared and began to climb the long, 14-story ladder up to the open entry hatch. When the chief engineer checked over the latest computer print-out and waved the orange "GO" flag, the man slowly closed the open hatch and carefully locked it. Then the final countdown began.

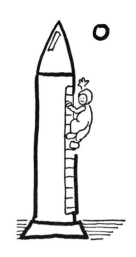

The cold November wind whistled and moaned as it shook the dead weeds in the fenced garden in front of the abandoned mansion. Wooden shutters banged noisily against the windows as the wintry wind tried to tear them off their half-broken hinges, and the tattered, rotting walls seemed to shudder as the icy fists of the storm beat against them. A cold driving rain poured from the cloudy, forbidding sky, turning the deserted garden into a sullen black lake that slowly and menacingly crept up to the crumbling concrete steps, while dead leaves floated like ghostly ships in the rising waters. A yellow flashing streak of lightning roared out of the sky and hit an old dead oak tree beside the house. The stricken tree quivered and rocked back and forth on its rotten roots. Slowly, slowly and silently, it began to fall.

On a sunny spring morning, the huge giant walked softly through his lovely garden. Suddenly, he spied a golden bird perched on the lowest limb of a blooming shrub. The bird was singing a sweet melody that reminded the giant of his early years. He rushed toward the shrub with nothing but kindness in his heart. His approach frightened the startled bird and caused him to soar into the sky. The giant stopped still on the path and called to the bird to return, but to no avail.

PURPOSE: Context clues

PREPARATION
1. Gather the following materials.
   —envelopes   —paper   —pencils
   —sentence strips   —box with top

2. Make up twelve to twenty sentences composed of words that can be rearranged to make a whole sentence without using one of the words. (The sentences on the following page may be used for starters.)

3. Cut the sentences apart into cards with only one word on each card.

4. Put the cards for each sentence in an envelope. Number each envelope.

5. Put the envelopes, paper and pencils in a box for learning center or seat work use. Print the following directions inside the box top, and print the rearranged sentences on the bottom of the box for an answer key.

PROCEDURE
1. Take one envelope out of the box at a time. Spread the words out, and form a sentence with them.

2. When you have made a sentence, rearrange the words to form a new sentence without using **one** of the words. (Omit only **one** word.)

   Example: There was a princess inside that pumpkin.
             A princess was inside that pumpkin. (**There** is not used.)

3. Copy the new sentences onto a sheet of paper.

4. Continue until you have rearranged all the sentences. Then check your new sentences with the answer key on the back of the box.

5. Return all word cards to the envelopes as they are used, and place the envelopes back in the box.

Drop A Word

1. The clown then jumped into the tank full of water.

2. Surprisingly enough people came to the party from many lands.

3. The funniest thing happened on the way to that softball game.

4. Some dogs and cats were fighting in the alley.

5. The sun's glare gave eerie light to the whole scene.

6. The snow in winter makes northern life difficult.

7. I am already in the school choir.

8. The story is being told all around town.

9. I just can't understand why you will agree to go.

10. The concert last night was really a great one.

11. The dark sky was becoming forbidding.

12. There was an elephant in that cage.

13. The parade route wound around the corner and down the block.

14. Aren't you going to go with your friends?

15. From a great distance came the sound of music.

GRAMMAR-CRACKER CAKE

Nouns and verbs and other parts of speech are recipe ingredients for sentences. They must be combined correctly so that a sentence will present a whole thought.

Read the recipe directions below. Tell what part of speech each underlined word is by writing its name in the crossword puzzle.

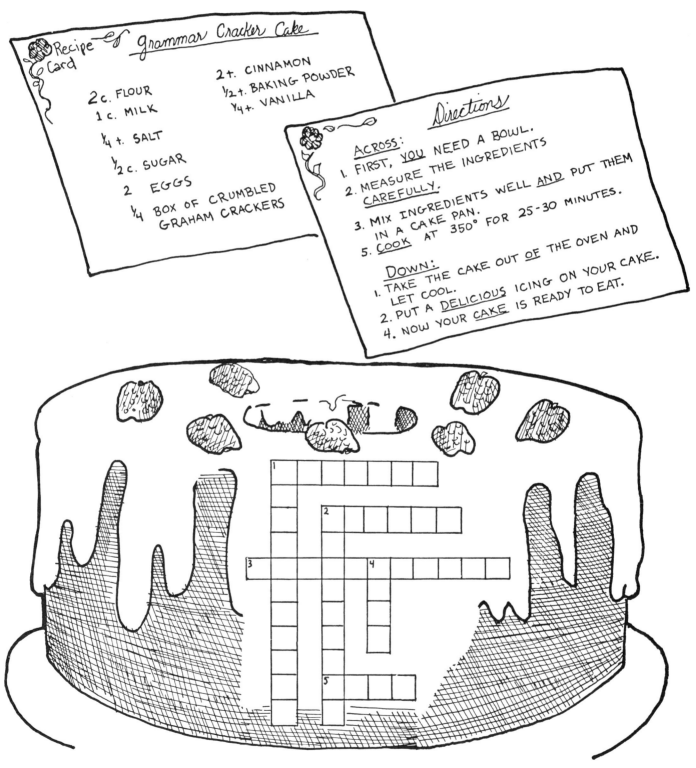

CLASSIFICATION TUMBLE

All these packages came tumbling into the Classification Center. Please help restore order by drawing a line through the word in each package that does not belong, and writing a classification word for the remaining words on the line below each package. (Use your dictionary for help if you need it.)

Example:

yacht
canoe
~~airplane~~
tug

__boats__

parka
snood
muffler
brochure

encyclopedia
abacus
dictionary
atlas

poultry
pastry
parrot
pasta

weasel
cobra
angora
aardvark

kale
zucchini
kumquat
broccoli

castle
cabin
poncho
mansion

humid
freezing
sultry
dusty

Asia
Canada
England
Mexico

yard
gallon
pint
quart

Plants   Oceans   Fruits

Print words to fill in the three packages above.

TIME FLIES

Time flies—especially when we're doing something we like!

On the clock face below, you should find 21 words related to the passage of time. Circle each word, and write it on the grandfather clock below.

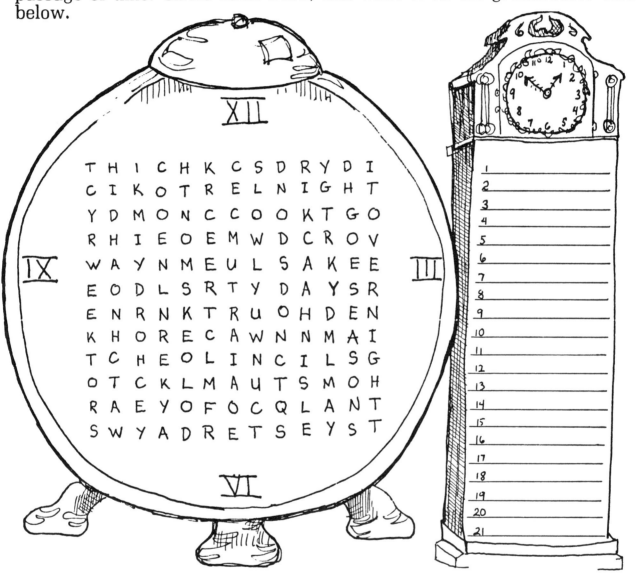

1. Name something you can read in one minute. _____

2. Name two things you can write in one hour. _____ _____

3. Name something you need a week to do. _____

4. Use the back of this sheet to write a paragraph telling about one of the following:
   —a world without calendars . . .
   —the day all the clocks were two hours fast . . .
   —the magic wristwatch . . .

On The Flip Side

PURPOSE: Understanding multiple meanings

PREPARATION

1. Cut records shapes from black construction paper.

2. Use white chalk or crayon to print on each record a word that has several meanings.

   Examples: trunk   light
              run   up
              back   turn
              set   order

3. Provide white chalk or crayons and the Procedure directions for student use.

PROCEDURE

1. Draw pictures to show different meanings of the word on the record.

2. "Flip" the record, and write one sentence using each meaning of the word.

"SEYMOUR THE ELEPHANT USED HIS TRUNK TO LOAD HIS CLOTHES TRUNK INTO THE TRUNK OF HIS CAR."

PAIR UP

PURPOSE: Using homonyms

PREPARATION
1. Gather the following materials.
   —game cards
   —scissors
   —red pen
   —green pen

2. Cut the following page to make nine sets of homonym cards and an illustration for one word in each of the sets (only one word is illustrated, not both).

3. Make a red X on one word in each pair, and a green X on the other.

4. Make three stacks of cards—one with red X's, one with green X's and one with illustrations.

PROCEDURE
1. This game is for two players.

2. The three stacks of cards are placed in the middle of the table.

3. Divide one stack of word cards equally between the two players. The other two stacks remain in the center of the table.

4. The first player draws a card from the word card stack. If this card matches a card in his/her hand, player places the pair on the table in front of him/her and draws another card. If not, he/she may keep that card, and must add one card from his/her hand to the bottom of the word stack on the table.

5. The next player takes a turn and repeats the same procedure.

6. Each time a player gets a pair, he/she may draw a card from the stack of illustrations. If the illustrations matches any pair the player has on the table, he/she may keep it and add it to the pair. If not, he/she may add it to her/his hand, and add another card to the bottom of the stack from his/her hand (either word or illustration stack, depending on which is discarded).

7. The first person to make five pairs or to get two pairs with matching illustrations wins the game.

PAIR-UP

pen	pin	
scent	cent	
pair	pear	
plane	plain	
flour	flower	
waist	waste	
root	route	
steak	stake	
foul	fowl	

THE LEANING TOWER OF PAIRS

PURPOSE: Using synonyms, antonyms and homonyms

PREPARATION

1. Enlarge and reproduce the "Leaning Tower of Pairs" game board. Glue it into a file folder, or put it on tagboard.

2. Cut out 120-140 tagboard squares to make 60-70 pairs of synonym, antonym and homonym cards. Write the words on the cards.

3. Place the cards in the folder, and make the game available for individual student use. Provide a clock or timer for the game.

4. Write the following directions on the front of the folder.

PROCEDURE

1. This game is a race against the clock. Set the timer for the specified time, and begin.

2. Turn 20 cards face up on the table.

3. Find a synonym, antonym or homonym pair, and place these two cards on the tower, beginning at the bottom left corner and working from left to right. Continue to do this with all the pairs you can make with the first 20 cards.

4. Drawing one more card at a time, pair all the cards and place them in the tower. Try to fill the entire tower before your time runs out.

5. When your time has expired, count the pairs you have placed in the tower. On the back of the folder, record your name, the number of pairs placed and how much time you used. Challenge a classmate to beat your time.

78

HETTIE HARNESSES HETERONYMS

Help Hettie Heteronym harness the heteronyms that have been left out of this story. Use these heteronym words to fill in the blanks to complete the story:

> read
> live
> tear
> record

Then use these heteronyms and/or others in a creative ending that you write to finish the story.

> close
> project
> refuse
> wind

A HETERONYM IS A WORD SPELLED LIKE ANOTHER WORD, BUT IS PRONOUNCED DIFFERENTLY AND HAS A DIFFERENT MEANING.

Hettie Heteronym had a marvelous new book to _____. It was a sequel to the one she had _____ last week. Last week's book had been about a _____ dog and a stuffed cat. In the story, the dog had gone to _____ with a new master, and the cat had been sent along to keep him company. The former owner had been sad to see the dog go, and could not resist shedding a _____ or two. When Hettie finished the book, she sympathized with the wear and _____ brought about by the dog's separation from his master.

Now Hettie was ready to begin the new book. She put her favorite _____ on the turntable and curled up on the sofa. She could hardly wait to find out what kind of adventure the author would _____ in this new book.

A GOOD VOCABULARY HELPS

PURPOSE: Using content area vocabulary

PREPARATION
1. Gather the following materials.
    —five flat boxes (hoisery or
        handkerchief boxes are fine)
    —felt pens
    —construction paper in 5 colors
    —3″ x 5″ index cards

2. Cover the boxes with construction paper and decorate to look like books. Use felt pens to write these words as titles on the "books."
    —Social Studies
    —Math
    —Science
    —Music
    —Art

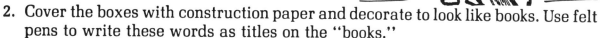

3. On the cards, print words associated with each of these content areas appropriate to the grade level of the students. To make this activity self-checking, place dots corresponding to the different colors of construction paper on each box on the backs of the cards.

    Examples:

4. Place the boxes and all the word cards in a learning center, or assign as an independent activity.

PROCEDURE
1. Sort cards and place them in the appropriate boxes.

MATH MIX-UP

You'll be much better in math if you can recognize and use math terms and their meanings.

Match these word beginnings and endings to find common math terms.

	Word Beginnings	Word Endings
1.	ADD	—O
2.	TRI	—ION
3.	ME	—TION
4.	EQUAT	—IO
5.	ZER	—TRACTION
6.	SPH	—ANGLE
7.	REC	—PH
8.	PER	—DUCT
9.	MULTIP	—TRIC
10.	DEC	—END
11.	SUB	—ERE
12.	DIV	—TANGLE
13.	FRAC	—LICATION
14.	DE	—IMAL
15.	QUOT	—IDE
16.	GRA	—GREE
17.	RAT	—IENT
18.	SQ	—AGE
19.	AVER	—CENT
20.	PRO	—UARE

Number a separate sheet of paper from 1 to 20. Write the words you have just made. Make a check (✓) beside any you don't know the meaning of, and look them up in your dictionary.

MATH WITH MEANING

Now let's use those math words. Fill in each of these blanks with a word from this math vocabulary list. Use each word only once.

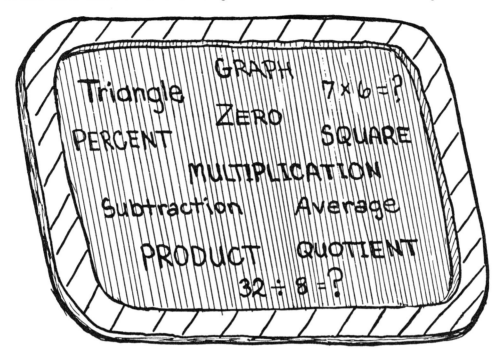

1. A _____ is a three-sided polygon.

2. If all the members of your class are present, the attendance will be 100 _____ and perfect.

3. A drawing showing relationships between sets is known as a _____.

4. _____ is an operation for computing repeated addition.

5. If you divided 63 by 9, 7 would be the _____.

6. _____ is the number of members in an empty set.

7. ☐   This is a _____.

8. The sum of a set of numbers divided by the number of addends is known as the _____.

9. When you multiply 9 times 9, 81 is the _____.

10. When one addend and the sum are known, the operation used to find the missing addend is _____.

HERE'S LOOKING AT YOU

Draw a picture of yourself here. You may make it realistic or cartoon-type. Think about the features that make you special, and try to show them.

Write five words that you think could be used to describe how you look. Look up each of the words in your dictionary (after you have written them, please!) to check the spellings and meanings. Write the dictionary page number beside each word.

Word	Page No.
1. _____	_____
2. _____	_____
3. _____	_____
4. _____	_____
5. _____	_____

Now, write one word that you feel "sums up" the word picture you have painted of yourself. Write the word and its full meaning from the dictionary.

_____

_____

_____

_____

Does the word mean exactly what you thought it did? _____

Write only three words to describe your personality. Then look them up in the dictionary to check spellings and meanings. Beside each word, write the number of dictionary meanings given. You may find that your personality is more complicated than you thought!

1. _____

2. _____

3. _____

Circle the word below that you think best sums up your personality.

complex   gregarious   dynamic

Look that word up in the dictionary and use the meaning to help you write a short paragraph to explain yourself to the world.

_____

_____

_____

_____

DAYS TO REMEMBER

Fill in the blanks with words from the list that best describe the days.

brisk	blistering	balmy	frightening	cloudy	comforting
bright	beautiful	snowy	marvelous	early	sweltering
dry	shining	darker	gloomy	lonely	rain-parched
sad	quiet	stormy	rainy	eerie	glorious

1. I looked out the window to see the sun shining, the birds singing and the flowers blooming. Oh, what a _____, _____, _____ day!

2. Thunder roared, lightning flashed and the _____ day became even _____ and more _____.

3. Imagine the children's surprise when they awoke to a _____, _____ and _____ Christmas Day.

4. It will take more than a _____, _____ day to dampen the fourth graders' enthusiasm for their picnic.

5. All the townspeople gathered for a bonfire on that _____, _____ autumn evening.

6. Since her faithful kitty had been run over, Sandy's day turned into a _____ and _____ one.

7. The calm before the storm made the day seem strangely _____ and _____.

8. The dust storm added one more unpleasant event to the _____, _____, _____ day.

9. The _____, _____ day finally gave way to a _____, _____ night.

85

Find the first food listed in your dictionary. Write the name of the food and the page number on which you found it.

_____   _____

Find the last vegetable listed in your dictionary. Write that word and the words on either side of it in these blanks.

_____   _____   _____

The words below are all ways to prepare meat. Look up the meaning of any you don't know, and write the meaning for each in your own words.

Broil —_____

Sauté —_____

Fry —_____

Braise —_____

Sear —_____

Boil —_____

Bake —_____

Which of these would you use to cook a turkey? _____

Find the definition for "calorie" in your dictionary. According to this definition, how many calories do you think you should have each day? _____

Write a good definition for the word "gourmet."

_____

_____

Make a menu for a gourmet meal you'd really like for your next birthday. Look up any words you don't know how to spell.

DINER'S KNOW-HOW

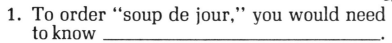

People are eating out more all the time. One recent report shows that one out of every three food dollars is spent on food eaten away from home.

Can you read a menu and tell what you will really be getting for your money? Use a reference book for help in completing this "Diner's Know-How" sheet.

1. To order "soup de jour," you would need to know _____.

2. How are "table d'hôte" and "à la carte" different? _____
   _____
   _____

3. Name four beverages you might order. _____
_____

4. A "quiche" is _____.

5. "Stir-fried vegetables" are _____
_____ .

6. "Souffles" are made by _____
_____ .

7. The difference between "boiled" and "broiled" is _____
   _____
   _____ .

8. A tossed green salad is usually made from _____,
   _____ and _____.

9. "Burger" is short for _____;
   "shake" is short for _____,
   and "fries" are really _____
   _____ .

10. At the end of every perfect meal, there's the "gratuity." What does this mean? _____

87

FEELING FINDERS

PURPOSE: Associating words with feelings

PREPARATION

1. Reproduce copies of the "Feeling Finders" work sheet on the following page.

2. Cut along the lines to make fifteen word cards.

3. Place the cards in unsealed envelopes, and distribute to students.

4. Make available the Procedure directions and a good collection of books appropriate for the students' reading interests portraying strong character and personality traits in a variety of settings.

PROCEDURE

1. Write your name and the date on the front of the envelope.

"ASTOUNDED"

2. Read the word on each card, and try to remember a time when you felt like the word on the card. Think about the circumstances that caused you to feel that way.

3. Look through books on the reading table to find a sentence that shows a story character experiencing the same feeling.

4. Write the sentence, the name of the character, the title of the book and the page number on the back of the word card. Here's an example:

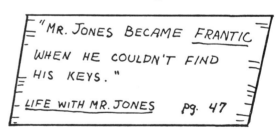

"MR. JONES BECAME FRANTIC WHEN HE COULDN'T FIND HIS KEYS."

LIFE WITH MR. JONES   Pg. 47

5. Continue until you have completed all of the cards. Seal the envelopes and add the date on which you finished to the front.

6. Place the envelope in the box on the reading table to be opened at a given time when examples will be shared and discussed.

ASTOUNDED

DEJECTED

ELATED

JOYFUL

EXHAUSTED

MISERABLE

ECSTATIC

REGRETFUL

FRANTIC

OVERWHELMED

FURIOUS

IMPATIENT

WEARY

HORRIFIED

EXCITED

The nicest greeting cards of all are ones that are especially designed and made by hand for a special person.

Match words and phrases from the two columns below to make messages to send for each of the occasions listed. Write each message on the line beside the appropriate occasion.

Sending . . .	. . . concern
May this be . . .	. . . happy thoughts
Please accept . . .	. . . the best one yet
Sincere ..	. . . special wishes
Thinking . . .	. . . congratulations
Offering . . .	. . . you well
Wishing . . .	. . . my appreciation

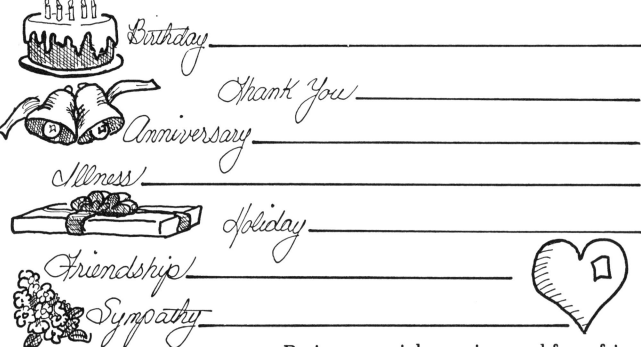

Birthday _____

Thank You _____

Anniversary _____

Illness _____

Holiday _____

Friendship _____

Sympathy _____

Design a special occasion card for a friend, and write your own message in five words or less.

SHOW YOUR FEELINGS

Find at least 40 words that express a mood or a feeling in the word-find puzzle below.

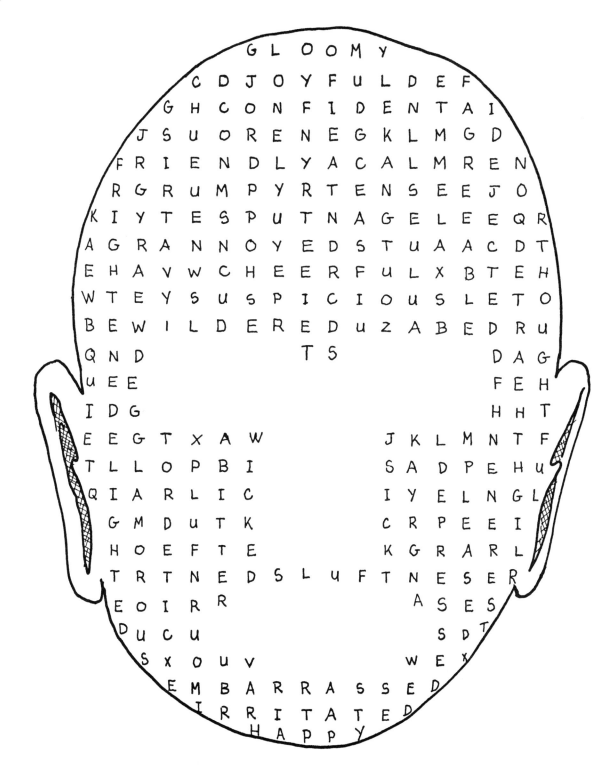

Add facial features, hair and anything else you like to make the face show a feeling or a mood.

AN ORANGE IS AN ORANGE . . .

PURPOSE: Forming sensory impressions

PREPARATION

    1. Provide an orange, paper, pencils and crayons for each student.

    2. Give the following directions to the students.

PROCEDURE

    1. Take two minutes to look at, feel, smell and study your orange.

    2. List at least 10 words that describe the orange.

    3. Write the names of three food dishes that may be made with oranges or orange juice.

    4. Make up a brand new recipe using oranges. Write the recipe on a sheet of paper, and illustrate it in color.

OR

Describe a new and creative way to use oranges. Draw and color a picture to illustrate the use.

    5. After all your work is done, the next agenda item is an orange snack time, of course!

Birds of a Feather do What?

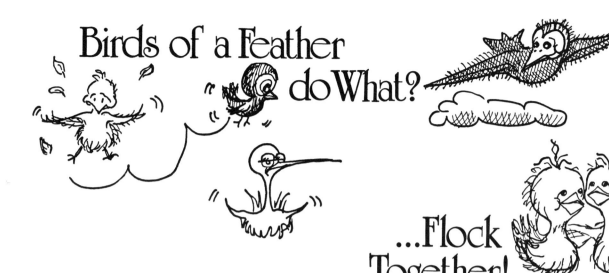

...Flock Together!

In the fewest words possible, write what you think each of these sayings means.

A fool and his money are soon parted.

_____

All that glitters is not gold.

_____

A little knowledge is a dangerous thing.

_____

Don't count your chickens before they hatch.

_____

Early to bed, early to rise, makes a man healthy, wealthy and wise.

_____

A bird in the hand is worth two in the bush.

_____

Select one of the sayings above. Copy it on a separate sheet of paper, and illustrate it to make a poster for your room.

SENSATIONAL SENTENCES

PURPOSE: Interpreting and conveying
sensations suggested by words

PREPARATION

1. Reproduce copies of the "Sensational Sentences" work sheet for the students.

2. Provide a copy of the Procedure directions for student use.

PROCEDURE

1. Combine one word or phrase from each of the three columns to make as many sentences as possible. Words and phrases may be used more than once so long as they are not used twice in the same sentence combination.

2. Check to make sure your sentences are complete and correct.

3. Select five of your sentences to illustrate in the margin or at the bottom of the page.

IN THE DISTANCE, A DOG HOWLED WEARILY.

I	II	III
Sparkled with sunshine	The unicorn is	Gregariously
Most of the time	My teacher smiled	Triumphant
Before dawn	The king marched	A sinking feeling
At half past eight	Winners are	Classically elegant
On the bright side	A dog howled	Guilty
Yesterday	My sister looked	Fiercely proud
As the whistle blew	Kittens purr	Desperately lonely
Every now and then	The patient reported	Lively and alert
After dinner	Film stars appear	Contentedly
In the distance	A baby clapped	Joyfully
From day to day	Grandmother rocked	Wearily

Sentences

1. _____

2. _____

3. _____

4. _____

5. _____

6. _____

7. _____

8. _____

9. _____

10. _____

11. _____

HUE ME IN!

PURPOSE: Interpreting and conveying moods created by words

PREPARATION

1. Write a different descriptive phrase or sentence conveying an environmental mood on sheets of drawing paper (one sheet for each student).

   Examples to use:

   The rutted, rocky road led through the tall, menacing mountains which were covered with huge trees and overgrown shrubs.

   . . . dusty, dark trail through the deep forest . . .

   . . midnight, the mysterious and malevolent witching hour . . .

   An eerie stillness spread over the city sidewalks . . .

   The bright sunshine seemed to illuminate the vivid sky, and bring a touch of sheer magic to the desert sunset.

2. Fold the sheets, and distribute one to each student as you give them the Procedure directions orally.

PROCEDURE

1. Students read the descriptive passage and select only one crayon to use to illustrate it.

2. The object is to use the crayon in varying levels of intensity and shading to convey the mood and feel of the description.

3. Sharing and discussing the impressions and completed illustrations are important aspects of this activity.

HOLIDAY CHECK-UP

Have you checked your holiday vocabulary lately? Here's a little test to help you do just that.

1. Draw a line from the name of each holiday to the name of the symbol that is associated with it.

2. Fill in the missing vowels in the words.

3. Then draw a line to the picture of another symbol for the same holiday. (Use your dictionary for help if you need it.)

One holiday is done for you. You do the rest.

m_tz_s

N_w Y__r's D_y

r_bb_t

St. P_tr_cks D_y

w_tch

l_v_

Ch_n_K_h

l_pr_ch__n

Ind__n

l_tk_

E_st_r

Th_nksg_v_ng

mistletoe

r_s_l_t__ns

Christmas

H_ll_w__n

V_l_nt_n_'s D_y

P_ss_v_r

97

ON THE WORD TRACK

PURPOSE: Seeing relationships between words

PREPARATION

1. Print one of the category words below (or substitute your own) on each railroad car. Then reproduce a copy for each student.

Categories

mood	weight	careers	holidays
size	color	animals	weather
age	time	plants	transportation

2. Provide dictionaries and a thesaurus for student use.

3. Place in a learning center setting, or use as seat work or home work.

98

ON THE WORD TRACK

Fill each railroad car with words related to the category word. If you think of more words than you can fit in the space, write the category word on the back of your paper, and list the rest of your words under it.

AUTHOR SAVVY

Practice a little "Author Savvy" by substituting more exciting words from the list below for the words underlined in the story. Rewrite this story with the word substitutions. Use each word only once, and circle it so you will know it has been used. Give the story a more exciting title, and illustrate it.

The Empty House

When Alicia found that she was by herself in the big, empty house, her heart began to beat quickly. She called for help, but her only answer was a strange quiet. Her walk echoed as she moved through the empty hallway to the top of the stairs. She stopped and tried to look through the white fog that filled the house to see what was at the bottom of the stairs, but everything was foggy. Her legs shook as she made herself to walk down the stairs. When she came to the landing, she sat down to rest. She was too scared to go on. Then something dark moved at the bottom of the stairs. Alicia was too afraid to take a breath. She heard something coming toward her, something that had sharp feet that clicked on every step. She pushed against the railing. Whatever it was had just about found her. She heard a quiet sound, and felt something cold run over her arm. Afraid of the worst, she looked up finally, and then put out her arms. A warm furry body climbed into her lap and licked her shoulder. Alicia laughed out loud. It was her own dog Oscar. She wasn't by herself anymore. She and Oscar got up and ran down the rest of the steps and out the front door into the daylight. They were fine at last!

Words to Use

deserted	bannister	sunshine	nuzzled	reverberated
giggled	snarl	moving	abode	frightened
footsteps	realized	puppy	icy	indistinct
pointed	farther	base	steps	stairway
alone	trail	isolated	fearing	terrified
suddenly	nails	paced	huge	mansion
jumped	peeked	shrank	head	shadowy
vacant	raced	at last	foot	trembled
fuzzy	almost	forced	peer	staircase
reached	descend	paused	mist	ghostly
pound	sank	crept	held	discovered
breathe	safe	reply	eerie	screamed
silence	low	each		

100

AUTHOR SAVVY

Practice a little "Author Savvy" by substituting more exciting words from the list below for the words underlined in the story. Rewrite this story with the word substitutions. Use each word only once, and circle it so you will know it has been used. Give the story a more exciting title, and illustrate it.

A Jungle Trip

As the group went into the deep jungle for a nine-day trip, they were surprised to hear a loud sound coming from behind a big tree. The leader hurried ahead to find himself looking into the bright eyes of a large, mean tiger with a wide mouth, sharp teeth and a hungry look about it. With one quick jump and a loud sound, the tiger ate the leader. Deciding that the man was a good bite, the tiger smelled the air, looking for more people to eat. Following the smell, he ran straight toward the scared people to go on with his meal. Acting quickly, a man got a gun and pointed it at the tiger. He pulled the trigger, and there was a big bang! Smoke was in the air. When it went away, the scared people looked at the place where the tiger had been. They were surprised to see nothing there. All that was left of the tiger was a yellow and brown striped hammock tied between two trees. "Oh, dear," said the man. "What I was aiming for was a tiger-skin carpet!"

Word List

ravenous	startled	tremendous	consume	caravan
dense	glowing	resounding	continue	forward
travellers	safari	frightened	scanned	golden
hostile	rushed	devoured	ferocious	echoing
peering	roar	cavernous	delicious	pounce
sniffed	morsel	razor-edged	grabbed	amazed
remained	shooting	cinnamon	feast	filled
explosion	hanging	trembling	cleared	scent
squeezed	rifle	aimed	sighed	rug
snarl	sped	swiftly	area	huge

BOBBY'S HOBBIES

PURPOSE: Practice in double letters

PREPARATION

1. It would be helpful (but not necessary) to provide a list of words with double letters for reference.

2. Choose a leader. Make certain the leader understands that "Bobby" likes words with double letters and doesn't like words that don't include double letters.

PROCEDURE

1. The leader gives the following explanation to the group.

"Bobby is a bright student who is interested in lots of different things. In fact, there are so many things Bobby likes that we could probably name hundreds! There are also many things that Bobby doesn't like. I'll tell you some things Bobby likes and some he doesn't like. You try to figure out why some words are in the "like" category and other words go in the "dislike" category. I'll give you one hint: pay close attention to the words, and try to visualize them."

The leader starts with the following examples and continues to give examples until all students figure out the game. As other students understand the game, they may join the leader in giving examples to the remaining participants.

2. The leader starts with the following examples and continues to give examples.

Bobby likes gr<u>ee</u>n, but he doesn't like blue.
Bobby like pe<u>pp</u>er, but he doesn't like salt.
Bobby likes baseba<u>ll</u>, but he doesn't like hockey.

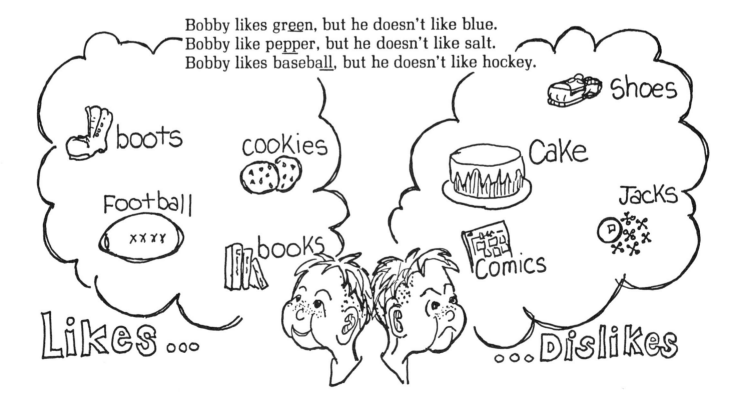

102

CONSTRUCTION CREW

All newspaper reporters know that every news article should include information on who, when, where and what happened. The really good reporters add enough descriptive words or phrases to give the writing "pizzazz" to hold the reader's attention.

Each of these sentences tells something that happened to someone. In other words, you have the "who" and the "what." Add one word or phrase from each column below to make the simple, unexciting sentences more interesting. Use each word or phrase only once.

Where	When	"Pizzazz"
on another planet	last Sunday	bewitching
at the beach	on the stroke of 12	gorgeous
on a city street	just before dark	magnificient
at the cave's entrance	a year ago today	hideous
in the garden	yesterday	unrealistic
at the museum	week before last	glamorous
over the rainbow	at dawn	heartbreaking

1. She bought the blouse.

   _____

2. We saw the sunset.

   _____

3. I lost my kite.

   _____

4. He heard that screech.

   _____

5. Mother smelled a rose.

   _____

6. The girl's tears fell.

   _____

7. She heard the news.

   _____

WORD OF THE DAY

PURPOSE: Word appreciation

PREPARATION

1. You will need the following materials.
   - —chalkboard
   - —pencils
   - —paper

2. Each morning, write a "Word of the Day" on the chalkboard. Use one of the following, or any of your own.

light	snow	boat	coat
rain	school	sun	night
day	house	fire	life

PROCEDURE

1. During the day, make a list of as many words as you can that contain the "Word of the Day." Hyphenated or double words may be used.
   Examples: raincoat   rainbow
   raindrop   rain hat
   At the end of the day, compare lists to see who has the most words.

2. Or, write as many words as you can that have the same ending sound as the "Word of the Day."

3. Or, write a story using the "Word of the Day" as many times as possible.

4. Or, try to find the word in everything you read all day long (texts and library books, newspapers, classroom charts, etc.). Make a list of all the times you find it. Give the sources and page numbers.

PRESENTING a PAL

PURPOSE: Word usage and appreciation

PREPARATION

1. Explain to the students that the object of this activity is to use as many words as possible that begin with the same letter as the first letter of a student's first name.

2. Provide pencils and paper for students to use to make notes if necessary as they talk together about their introductions.

Examples:

Find out about Fantastic Fred. Fred is a fine, fashionable friend. He can fix fascinating fancies and fetch ficticious fantasies all because of his futuristic foresight and far-reaching imagination.

Meet my mighty friend Matt. Matt mixes majestically with a majority of mankind. He may be our masterful mayor because of his many, magnificent talents.

PROCEDURE

1. Choose a partner, Make up an introduction for your partner to present him/her to the class following your teacher's instructions.

2. Take turns introducing each other.

Write a story about Vicki and Victor's visit to Vacation Village. Use as many **V** words in the story as you can.

_____

_____

_____

_____

_____

_____

_____

_____

_____

_____

_____

_____

Word List
(Use your
dictionary
to find
more.)
villa
vacancy
voyage
vague
villager
valid
vagabond
vehicle
visitor
vegetable
vice
vain
very
vinegar
vanguard

WORD USAGE SKILLS COMPETENCY REVIEW

Read this paragraph carefully.

1. The cold November wind whistled and moaned as it shook the dead weeds in the fenced garden in front of the abandoned mansion. 2. Wooden shutters banged noisily against the windows as the wintry wind tried to tear them off their half-broken hinges, and the tattered, rotting walls seemed to shutter as the icy fists of the storm beat against them. 3. A driving rain poured from the cloudy, forbidding sky, turning the deserted garden into a sullen, black lake that slowly and menancingly crept up to the crumbling concrete steps, while dead leaves floated like ghostly ships in the rising waters. 4. A flashing yellow streak of lightning roared out of the sky and hit an old dead oak tree beside the house. 5. The stricken tree quivered and rocked back and forth on its rotten roots. 6. Slowly, slowly and silently, it began to fall.

1. Find the words pictured. Write the correct word under each picture.

_____   _____   _____

2. Circle the word that would best help you understand the meaning of the word **wind** in sentence 1 of the story.

> November
> whistled
> front

3. Circle the four words in sentence 2 that tell about weather.

4. Circle the word that means the same thing as **dead** as it is used in sentence 1.

> deceased
> dying
> old

5. Circle the word that means the opposite of **dead** as it is used in sentence 1.

> pretty
> withered
> living

6. Circle the word that tells how the rain came from the sky.

> cloudy
> forbidding
> poured

7. Circle the word that best could be used to take the place of **silently** as it is used in sentence 6.

> noisily
> quietly
> quickly

8. Circle the word that would best describe how a child would feel in the stormy garden.

> carefree
> frightened
> contented

9. Draw a line under the four-word phrase in the paragraph that means the same thing as:

"It was raining cats and dogs."

10. Circle the word that best describes the mood suggested in sentence 3.

> eerie
> joyful
> pensive

11. In sentence 3, rain is to sky as plants are to:

> bouquets
> earth
> catalogs

12. Circle the word that does not describe the oak tree in sentence 4.

> yellow
> old
> dead

13. Circle the word that could best be used to replace **tried** in sentence 2.
> roared
> attempted
> stooped

14. Circle the word that could best be used to replace **crumbling** in sentence 3.

> sloping
> eroding
> creeping

15. Circle the word that could correctly be added to the end of sentence 6.

> into
> forward
> beside

16. Write the two words from sentence 3 that have double letters.

_____

_____

17. Circle the word that could be used in a poem to rhyme with **yellow.**

> follow
> mellow
> lowly

SKILLSTUFF

Comprehension Skills

III. COMPREHENSION SKILLS

_____ Can recall information read and select facts to remember

_____ Can read for a specific purpose

_____ Can find the main idea

_____ Can read to find details

_____ Can make comparisons and associations

_____ Can classify material read

_____ Can arrange ideas or events in sequence

_____ Can summarize

_____ Can read to verify answers

_____ Can draw conclusions

_____ Can make inferences

_____ Can predict outcomes

_____ Can make value judgments

_____ Can distinguish between

    _____ relevant and irrelevant

    _____ fact and opinion

    _____ cause and effect

_____ Is sensitive to author's purpose and mood

_____ Can identify with fictional characters

_____ Can identify character traits

_____ Is sensitive to the development of plot and sequence

_____ Can visualize

TIME
○
ON THE LINE

A time line records the important events in a person's life over a given period of time.

Select a person whose life interests you, and make a time line for that person. You may choose either a fictional character or a real person, but it must be a person whose life is written about in a book available to you. (At a later time, you may want to make a time line for a friend, your teacher or even yourself!)

Read the material about the person's life, and select six to eight important facts to record on the time line.

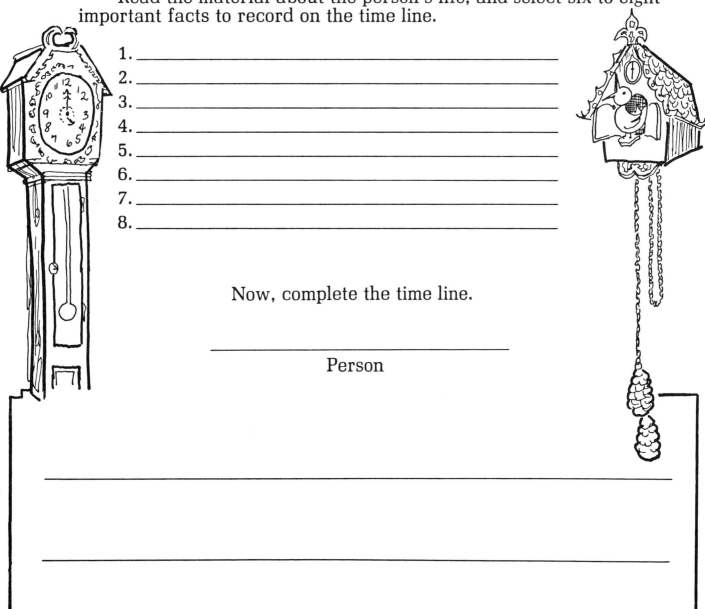

1. _____
2. _____
3. _____
4. _____
5. _____
6. _____
7. _____
8. _____

Now, complete the time line.

_____
Person

FRONT PAGE REVIEW

PURPOSE: Finding answers to specific questions

PREPARATION

1. Assemble enough newspapers for each student to have one.

2. Reproduce and distribute the work sheets, and provide a pencil for each student.

PROCEDURE

1. Follow the directions on the "Front Page Review" work sheet.

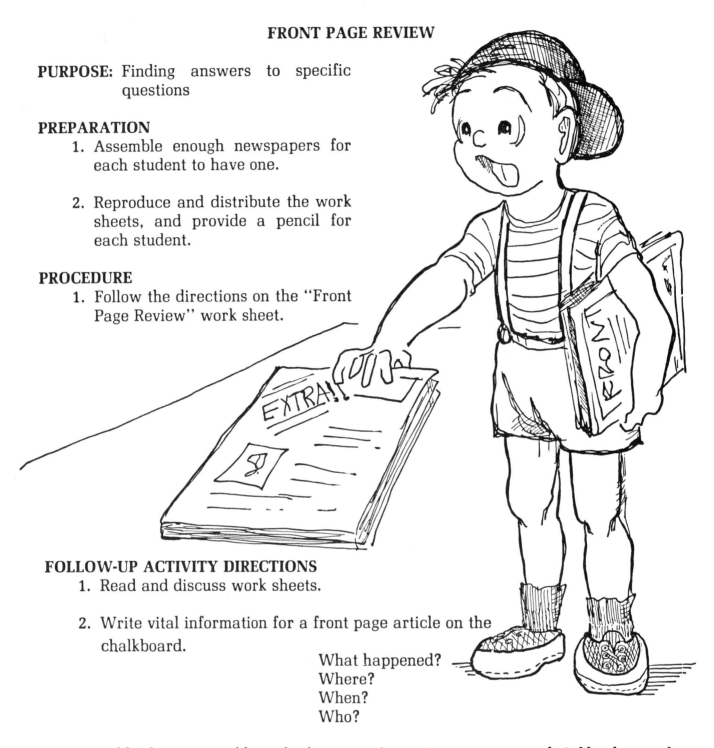

FOLLOW-UP ACTIVITY DIRECTIONS

1. Read and discuss work sheets.

2. Write vital information for a front page article on the chalkboard.

What happened?
Where?
When?
Who?

Add a few assorted bits of information (i.e.: witnesses, quotes, brief background information, etc.).

3. Direct students to write up the article, giving information as clearly and as concisely as possible.

4. Direct students to write headlines for their articles.

5. Share and compare the articles.

Front Page Review

Select an article from the front page of the newspaper.

1. Write the complete headline.
   _____

2. Read the entire article carefully.

3. Circle six key words in the article. Write them here.

   _____   _____   _____

   _____   _____   _____

4. Circle three key phrases. Write them here.

   _____
   _____
   _____

5. Whom does the article tell about?
   _____

6. What is the article about?
   _____

7. Where did the event take place?
   _____

8. Circle the one sentence that gives the main idea or carries the "punch line" of the article. Write the sentence.
   _____
   _____

9. Do you think the article tells everything it should? _____
   Why?
   _____
   _____

10. Do you think the headline really tells what the article is about, or is it misleading?
   _____

11. Write another headline for the article.
   _____

113

FUNNEL YOUR READING

PURPOSE: Using key words, phrases and topic sentences to get main idea

PREPARATION
1. Assign reading selections in content areas to students, and provide pencils and copies of the "Reading Funnel" work sheet for each student.

2. Assemble content materials to be read, and give any needed pre-reading directions (i.e.: new words, references to future use of material, etc.).

PROCEDURE
1. Read the assigned material carefully.

2. Reread and copy from the article any key words, key phrases and one main topic sentence in the proper spaces on the "Reading Funnel" work sheet.

3. Review the words, phrases and topic sentences. Use all three to help you write the main idea of the selection.

4. Write the name of the book and the page number at the bottom of the "funnel" for easy reference.

Note: After you have used this form enough to become familiar with it, you can adapt it to index cards for easier use when preparing reports or projects requiring more than one source of material.

READING FUNNEL WORK SHEET

Topic: _____

Key Words: _____

_____

Key Phrases: _____

_____

Topic Sentence or Sentences: _____

_____

_____

Main Ideas: _____

_____

_____

_____

_____

_____

Book:

_____

_____

_____

Page # _____

PEERING AT PARAGRAPHS

> Read the following paragraphs, and underline the topic sentence in each.

Marion was sitting on the front steps, enjoying the sun on her face. She looked up and down the street. Trees and bushes were beginning to turn green, and some early flowers were in bloom. Patches of grass were showing on the brown lawns. Down the block, some kids were playing baseball. Marion smiled. Spring had finally arrived.

Raindrops began to patter on the roof. The wind grew strong and began to roar about the house. Thunder crashed and boomed, and lightning sparkled and flashed its way across the sky. Gathering clouds blotted out the daylight, and the rain came down hard and thick. The storm we had been waiting for all day finally broke.

"I've looked everywhere for that book!" thought Tony. "I remember bringing it home and putting it on the counter. Then I took it into my bedroom to read after supper. I've looked on the counter, and it isn't there. I've searched the bedroom, and it isn't there. What could have happened to it?"

It was time for the party to begin. All the decorations were up; balloons and streamers were everywhere. The long table had flowers in the center and was loaded with food. A full punch bowl sat at one end of the table, and a giant cake filled the other. A big stack of beautifully wrapped presents was waiting, ready to be opened.

> Choose any of the above paragraphs. Write two more paragraphs for it. Your first paragraph must come before the chosen paragraph, and your second paragraph must follow it.

DETAIL DEDUCTION

Learning to read for details is an important skill for good readers. Practice using this skill by finding, circling and labeling the parts of the sentences below that tell "who," "what," "where," "when," "why" and "how."

Give yourself a reasonable time limit, and show off your "Detail Deduction" skills by finishing this sheet in that amount of time.

Example: (Jennifer) (worked to finish her chores) (in the garden) (quickly) (so that she could catch the train) (before noon.)

1. Walking along the beach at eventide, the little girl was carefully looking for shells and rocks for her collection.

2. Many people work very hard in hotels and restaurants just to gain experience while they are in management school.

3. The baby cried loudly because he had been left from dawn to dusk hungry and cold in his crib.

4. Danny the dog barked wildly outside the gate to signal the stranger's midnight arrival.

5. Even though the hunters became lost in the forest early in the day, they journeyed bravely on because of their concern for the lost dog.

6. Happily, Mrs. Andrews smiled as she sat on the porch in the morning sun to read the long letter from her friend.

TOPIC CENTERED

PURPOSE: Categorization/word association

PREPARATION

1. Write topics well known to students on sheets of drawing paper or newsprint. Provide a sheet for each student.

2. Fold the papers in half, and place in a basket.

PROCEDURE

1. Pass the basket, and allow each student to remove a folded sheet of paper.

2. Using a pencil and/or crayons, the students write as many words pertaining to the topic as possible in a specified time. Dictionaries may be used if necessary.

3. The student with the most correctly spelled words at the end of the specified time wins the game.

4. Allow time for the completed sheets to be illustrated to carry out the theme.

ADAPTATION

If a particular unit is being studied, all students may use the same unit-related topic. They might be asked to try for at least one word beginning with each letter of the alphabet, or for all three-syllable (or more) words, or the topic may be written on the chalkboard so that students may add words all during the day.

APPLE TREATS

Think about how many different ways we use apples. Add one extra word to each apple in the basket to make an apple treat. If you think of more ways to use apples than there are apples in the basket, draw in some extra ones!

apple

apple

apple

apple

apple

apple

apple

apple

apple

apple

apple

apple

apple

apple

apple

Write a recipe for an apple treat on the recipe card.

APPLES

ANALOGIES ON DEPOSIT

Find words in the safe to complete each sentence. Circle each word when you use it so that you will use each word only once.

1. Thorn is to rose as barnacle is to _____.

2. Tine is to fork as blade is to _____.

3. Petal is to flower as leaf is to _____.

4. Feather is to bird as fin is to _____.

5. Museum is to art as bank is to_____.

6. Necklace is to neck as ring is to _____.

7. Dust is to the desert as sand is to the _____.

8. Tooth is to a comb as rung is to a _____.

9. Shoe is to foot as glove is to _____.

10. Fur is to a cat as grass is to a _____.

11. A driver is to a bus as a pilot is to an _____.

12. A spoon is to a cook as a hammer is to a _____.

13. Day is to night as white is to _____.

14. A planet is to the sun as our moon is to the _____.

15. A roof is to a house as a top is to a _____.

16. A kitten is to a cat as a puppy is to a _____.

CINDERELLA'S CLOSET

Cinderella's closet is a mess! She's been kept so busy scrubbing floors and doing errands for her mean step-sisters that she has had little time for herself.

Help her get ready to leave with the prince by marking out the item in each box that does not fit.

121

PURPOSE: Classifying a variety of materials

PREPARATION
1. Arrange three sturdy paper bags upright and open on a table easily accessible to students.

2. Prepare any of the materials specified in the Procedure, and use accordingly.

PROCEDURE
1. A. Cut pictures from magazines of people obviously expressing emotions, and glue these to various colored construction paper circles.

B. Print emotion words (joyful, frantic, furious, etc.) on 3″ x 5″ cards.

C. Make signs for the bags, and hang them across the tops.

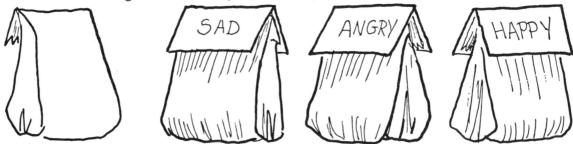

D. Students sort pictures and word cards into appropriate bags.

2. A. Cut stories from old basal readers, paragraphs from science and social studies books and sections from newspapers and magazines. Place these in a manila folder.

   B. Make signs for the classification bags.

   C. Direct students to sort reading materials into appropriate bags.

3. Use antonyms, homonyms and synonyms in the same manner.

4. Print phrases that tell "what," "when" or "where" on 3" x 5" cards, and use in the same manner.

5. For special unit or content area studies, and in at least a dozen other ways appropriate to you and your students, use the same method.

PURPOSE: Listing ideas in proper sequence.

PREPARATION

1. Cut out stories or articles from weekly classroom newspapers or magazines. Then cut the articles into sentence strips.

2. Place the sentence strips in envelopes, and label each with the title or main idea of the material.

3. Place the envelopes in a learning center or free work area, and provide paper, pencils and the following directions. (If working with children who need extra reinforcement, you may need to provide the uncut newspaper or magazine article for checking purposes.)

PROCEDURE

1. Read all the sentence strips carefully.

2. Select the main idea of the story or article first. Then order the sentences as you think they occurred originally in the article.

3. Write a one-paragraph summary of the story or article. Be sure to include all the important ideas in the order in which they occurred in the original story or article.

4. Compare your summary with one written by a classmate.

SEQUENCE OF EVENTS

PURPOSE: Sequencing

PREPARATION

1. Gather the following materials.
   —envelopes
   —comic strips
   —pencils and paper
   —box with top

2. Collect one-strip comics, or draw your own (with or without words).

3. Cut the strips apart, and place in an envelope. Prepare at least six or eight envelopes for variety.

4. Place all the envelopes in a box, and add pencils and paper. Print the following directions in the top of the box.

PROCEDURE

1. Take one envelope at a time from the box. Place all the frames from the comic strip before you, and look carefully at each one.

2. Arrange the frames in sequence to tell the story.

3. After you have done several, select one you like and draw another strip with exactly the same number of frames. Show what you think might have happened next.

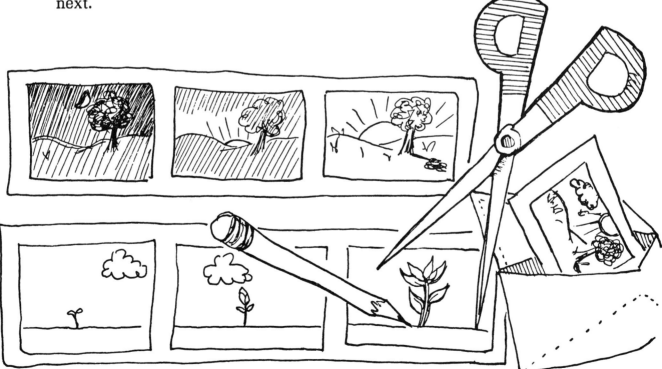

PURPOSE: Summarizing/getting main idea

PREPARATION
1. Reproduce copies of the "Special News Watch" work sheet on the following page.

PROCEDURE
1. Read each bulletin carefully.

2. Underline the important information that should be included in a special TV news flash.

3. Underline the single most important sentence twice.

4. Draw a circle around unnecessary sentences and phrases.

5. Rewrite the bulletin using as few words as possible.

NEWS BULLETIN

Just after noon today, three prisoners escaped from the State Prison located at 4609 Cumberland Circle East. These three prisoners are thought to be armed, and are considered very dangerous. At the time of their escape, they were wearing olive green prison uniforms. They escaped by hooking bed sheets together to make a rope to scale the prison wall. All three were serving 99-year sentences for murder and armed robbery. The prisoners are thought to be on foot, still together and seeking a way to get out of the state. Police helicopters joined in the search about two hours after the escape. All area residents are asked to be on the alert for these escaped prisoners, and to call local police at this number, 876-5429, if they have any reason to think they have spotted these people.

SPECIAL NEWS WATCH

SPECIAL NEWS FLASH

WEATHER BULLETIN

At 6 p.m. today, the United States Weather Bureau posted a special watch for the following states: Tennessee, Georgia, Florida, Virginia, North Carolina, South Carolina, Alabama, New York, Washington D.C., and parts of Pennsylvania and Delaware. Severe winds, heavy rainfall and electrical storms are predicted within the next twenty-four hours. As clouds build up and storm signals continue to develop off the East Coast, all area residents are advised to be alert for further news of storm warnings, flooding and a posted tornado watch. This storm appears to be similar in nature to last week's storm in the same area, and is expected to be equally severe.

SPECIAL NEWS FLASH

Fishy Facts Filmstrips

Many of the movies and filmstrips that you have seen were first written in book form. They were transferred into film for a variety of reasons, one of which is that lots of people remember what they see better than what they read.

Locate and read through several different souces of information about fish. Select at least 8 major facts that you have learned from your reading, and write these in complete sentences on the lines below.

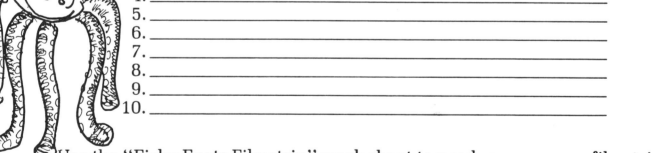

1. _____
2. _____
3. _____
4. _____
5. _____
6. _____
7. _____
8. _____
9. _____
10. _____

Use the "Fishy Facts Filmstrip" work sheet to produce your own filmstrip.

1. In the very first rectangle, write a title for your filmstrip. In the last rectangle, write "The End."

2. List one "Fishy Fact" in each rectangle. Write them in any style you choose, and add illustrations to each frame that will help the viewer to understand what you have written.

3. Show your filmstrip to classmates, and keep a log of their comments about your work.

FISHY FACTS FILMSTRIPS

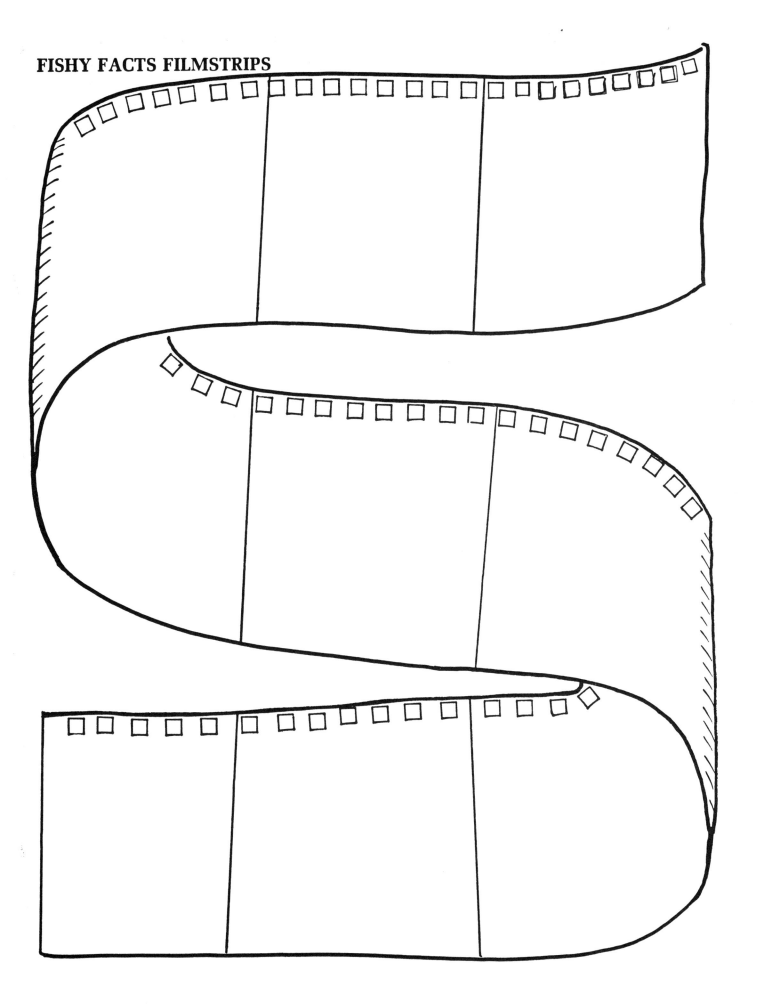

ABSOLUTELY ACCURATE ANSWERS

PURPOSE: Reading to verify answers

PREPARATION

1. Select a chapter or unit from a content area textbook (science, social studies, etc.). Write seven key words or phrases from the material on the "Absolutely Accurate Answers" work sheet.

2. Reproduce a copy of the work sheet for each student.

PROCEDURE

1. Ask students to read the content area material, giving attention to major topics and main ideas.

2. Distribute copies of the "Absolutely Accurate Answers" work sheet with instructions to follow the directions for completion.

3. After answers have been checked and scores determined, lead a follow-up discussion focused on the different types of reading skills needed for studying content area materials.

ABSOLUTELY ACCURATE ANSWERS

Without looking at your book, write the best definition you can for each of the following words or phrases.

1. _____

2. _____

3. _____

4. _____

5. _____

6. _____

7. _____

Now, reread the material carefully to check your answers. Be completely honest and determine your score. Give yourself
—10 points for each Absolutely Accurate answer . . . 5 points for Almost Accurate answers . . . 0 points for Inaccurate answers.

	Word	Absolutely Accurate	Almost Accurate	Inaccurate	Points
1.					
2.					
3.					
4.					
5.					
6.					
7.					

Total _____

THINK TANK

PURPOSE: Drawing conclusions

PREPARATION

1. Gather the following materials.
   —game board
   —24 3″ x 5″ index cards
   —timer
   —felt pen

2. Enlarge the game board on the following page.

3. Prepare two sets of cards, 12 to each set. On one card in each pair, write a "Think Tank" sentence. On the other, write a logical conclusion for that sentence. Mark each pair of cards with numbers, dots or any symbols to make this activity self-checking. Use these sentences for starters, if you like.

4. Place the game board in a free-time area in the classroom, and arrange the "Think Tank" cards face up around the board. Stack the conclusion cards inside the "Tank" in the center of the board.

PROCEDURE

1. Two players take turns drawing one card at a time and trying to match it with the proper "Think Tank" card on the board. The timer should be used, and if the card is not matched in a specified time, the player must put the card drawn on the bottom of the stack and forfeit that turn. If the card can be matched in the given time, the player picks up the "Think Tank" card and keeps the pair.

2. The game continues until all cards have been paired. The player with more pairs wins the game.

132

CONCLUDING CONCLUSIONS

Finish the following diagrams by "reading" them and drawing in picture "conclusions" in the spaces provided.

WHAT WILL HAPPEN?

PURPOSE: Drawing conclusions

PREPARATION

1. Gather the following materials.
   —fish bowl or other container
   —paper squares or index cards
   —felt pens

2. On each of the index cards, write an open-ended situation that would be of interest to the students.

PROCEDURE

1. Several students may play this game, or it may be used in a small reading group.

2. Sit in a circle and pass the bowl around to each participant.

Mrs. Smith was very angry because Tony was late for school. Tony explained to her that his mother was late for work, and he had to take his baby sister to the day care center. Mrs. Smith said, "You will have to tell that to the principal."

What will happen? What other solution could you see for the problem?

3. Each player reaches into the bowl and draws one card. Each student reads the card chosen to the group and explains what he/she thinks would be a logical conclusion.

4. The other players discuss the conclusion to determine if it is "logical," and if there are other logical conclusions. (Discussion and exchange of ideas are important features of this game.)

The factory workers asked for an extra coffee break because there was no air conditioning on the assembly line. The foreman said they were turning out less work already because of the hot weather, and the company could not afford another break.

What will happen next?

Betty and Sue had been friends for a long time. Their quarrel concerned a party to which Betty was invited and Sue was not. Sue felt that Betty should not go to the party, but Betty said that it had nothing to do with friendship, and she planned to go to the party.

Who is right?

AESOP'S WORKSHOP

Aesop was a slave in Greece over two thousand years ago. We still remember him for the fables he wrote and the lessons that they taught.

Read the following fables. Figure out what each one is trying to say, and write what you think is the "lesson" each teaches on the line below it.

The Cat and the Mice

Once there were some mice who were harassed by a cat. They held a meeting to decide what to do about it. One mouse stood up and said, "Since the cat moves so quietly, we can't hear it coming. If it had a bell tied round its neck, we would hear it ringing, and we could run to safety before it could catch us."

The other mice were delighted by this clever plan. But one old mouse stood up and said, "Yes, it's a good plan. But who is going to put the bell on the cat?"

The Boy and the Wolf

HELP! WOLF! WOLF!

There was a young boy who tended sheep in a village. Since he often found his job boring, he would create some excitement by running to the village and yelling "Wolf! Wolf!" as loud as he could. All the villagers would come running with tools and clubs to help him, only to find that he had played a trick on them, as there was really no wolf.

The boy thought this was funny, and did it several times. But one day, a real wolf actually did come out of the forest. This time, when the boy ran to the village calling, "Wolf!" no one came to help him. And the wolf ate all the sheep he wanted!

The Grasshopper and the Ant

It was winter, and the grasshopper was cold and hungry. He saw an ant eating some grains that had been stored during the summer, so he asked the ant to share his food.

"Didn't you store up some food last summer for the winter?" asked the ant.

"No," replied the grasshopper, "I was too busy singing then."

"Too bad," said the ant. "Since you sang all summer, you can just dance all winter!"

Choose one of the fables, and rewrite it in up-to-date language.

PREDICTION PUZZLES

Each story starter below presents a situation with several possible outcomes. Read the beginnings, and copy them on another sheet of paper. Then complete them by writing what your think will happen in each case.

Bertha and Alfred had been walking in the woods all afternoon. When the sun began to go down, they decided to head home. Alfred led the way down a path that wound around and suddenly ended in front of a high, wire fence.

"Hm," said Alfred uncertainly. "I was sure this was the right path to take. But I don't remember this fence."

"Oh, no," Bertha sighed, "don't tell me we're lost! And it's getting dark, too. What will we do?"

The kitty huddled against the building, trying to get out of the rain. It was cold and wet, and tired of being lost. The kitty meowed sadly. How it wished that it had a warm, dry home to go to.

Suddenly, the kitty saw a shadow and heard a person coming toward it.

Terry stretched and yawned as he woke up, wondering why he felt so uncomfortable. He opened his eyes and saw that his lamp was still on. Then he realized that he had slept in his clothes.

"Wow!" Terry groaned. "I must have fallen asleep last night when I was studying for my test! And now it's time to go to school, and I'm not ready! What am I going to do?"

"Be quiet," called Stanley as he closed the classroom door and hurried back to his seat. "She's coming down the hall now. Everybody get ready for the big surprise!"

Ms. Gregory walked in and sat down at her desk. "Good morning, class," she smiled. "How is everyone today?"

"Good morning, Ms. Gregory," replied the students. Then they called out, "Surprise! Happy Birthday! We brought you a cake! Surprise!!"

THE RIGHT THING TO DO

Sometimes it's hard to judge what is the right thing to do. Help the children in the situations below make the best possible judgments by telling what you think is the best thing to do in each case.

Craig had earned enough money from his dog-walking service to treat his friend Doug to the movies. He had invited Doug to go with him, and they were to meet at the theater at 1:30. At 12:00, Craig realized that if he paid Doug's way into the movie, there would not be enough money to buy popcorn and a drink for himself.

What should Craig do, and why?

_____

_____

_____

_____

Suzanne was having a very difficult time answering the questions on the history test. She hadn't studied enough, and was wishing that she could wave her pencil over her paper and make the correct words appear. Just then, she noticed that Greer was sneaking a look at his history book to find the answers.

What should Suzanne do, and why?

_____

_____

_____

_____

Barbara's family had just moved to town, and Barbara had not met any children her age. One day, Teddy saw Barbara playing alone and went over to meet her. They introduced themselves, and Barbara asked Teddy to play her new "Wacko-rama" game with her. Just as they started, Frank, Teddy's best friend, came up and wanted Teddy to come play with him instead.

What should Teddy do, and why?

_____

_____

_____

_____

IDENTIFY THE IRRELEVANTS

Draw a line through the sentence in each paragraph that does not belong.

Yesterday I went to the library to find a book of fairy tales. I looked through the shelves, and found one by Jakob and Wilhelm Grimm. There was another one by Hans Christian Andersen, and one called *The Blue Book of Fairy Tales*. My mother said we were going to have hamburgers for dinner. I checked out the book of fairy tales by Hans Christian Andersen.

Richard couldn't believe what he saw when he looked out of the window on the 25th of July. Snow was falling, covering the trees and flowers. Richard's sister Cheryl dropped her doll and began to cry. Richard watched the snowstorm in amazement. He wondered if he had somehow managed to sleep through the summer, so he checked the calendar, but it was still July. As he went back to the window, he shook his head in confusion and thought to himself, "I didn't know it could snow in July!"

Percival Prendergrast turned seven years old today. His mother and father gave him a new bicycle. His sister baked a cake for him. Percival's favorite color is green. His grandmother took him to a movie. At school, there was a party with ice cream and cookies to celebrate Percival's birthday. Percival had such a good time on his birthday that he decided to celebrate this same way every year.

My first swimming lesson was a real disaster! I was late to class because I wasted so much time in the dressing room. Then I got lost in the showers and couldn't find the pool. When I finally got there, I ran across to stand by my best friend, and the lifeguard blew the whistle at me to tell me not to run. I don't know how to whistle. When we were supposed to step carefully into the water, I slipped and fell in with a big splash. Then I tried to blow air out through my nose, but I choked, and the teacher had to come save me. After that, I just sat on the side and watched for the rest of the lesson.

ARE YOU SURE ABOUT THAT?

PURPOSE: Distinguishing between fact and opinion

PREPARATION

1. Reproduce copies of the "Opinionated Statements" work sheet.

PROCEDURE

1. Distribute copies of the "Opinionated Statements" work sheet.

2. Ask students to look over the work sheets. Lead a class discussion to set the scene for individual writing.

3. After work sheets are completed, ask students to work in small groups composed of those who selected a common topic.

4. After group discussion, each group should prepare a means of disproving the statement to the class. (This might be in the form of creative dramatics, panel discussion, written reports, cartoon series or any other presentation.) The emphasis here should be on originality and team work.

VARIATIONS

1. Ask students to work in groups to make lists of other "Opinionated Statements."

2. Assign the work sheet as home work, and ask students to discuss it with their families and prepare the three-paragraph paper as a project representative of family thinking.

3. Ask each student to bring in one newspaper or magazine article whose author's authority is in question. Mount all the articles on a bulletin board or chart to use in a learning center or skills lab setting.

140

Opinionated Statements

Sometimes it's hard to tell the difference between a fact and an opinion. This is especially dangerous when a little bit of factual information is used as the basis for much discussion and writing. People sometimes tend to believe almost anything they read.

Good readers need to learn to question the source of written material and the authority of the author in order to determine if the information really is factual.

Select one of the statements below, and write three paragraphs to disprove it. Write one paragraph telling why the statement is not true, and one paragraph telling how you think it may have started as an opinion and become accepted by some people as fact. Use the third paragraph to write an idea you'd like to develop as to the possible personal consequences of accepting the statements as factual.

Use dictionaries, encyclopedias or other reference materials if you need them.

1. Eskimos live in igloos.

2. All soldiers are strong and brave.

3. San Francisco is sliding into the ocean.

4. Actors lead very unhappy lives.

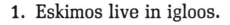 5. Flowers have sweet scents.

6. Dog owners are kind people.

7. Big business executives are not concerned about individual employees.

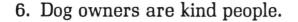

141

OPINIONATED OPHELIA

Opinionated Ophelia complained about a lot of things. Sometimes she complained about things just for the sake of complaining, and sometimes she complained because she had such very strong opinions.

Read the story below, and help Ophelia sort out facts and opinions.

Opinionated Ophelia woke up early on Monday morning. The sun was shining brightly, and her mother was already in the kitchen making breakfast. Her first thought was of the party she'd be attending that day, and how really stupid she thought Pat was to have the party at 3:00. Ophelia felt that 5:00 would be a much better time for a party, and that St. Patrick's Day was not a good party theme, anyway. Even though her mother had explained that Pat was born on St. Patrick's Day and that he thought a St. Patrick's Day theme was more exciting than a birthday theme, Ophelia still complained. She said that wearing green was a silly thing to do, that she didn't believe four-leaf clovers really brought good luck to the finder and that no one she knew had ever seen a leprechaun.

Her mother told her that St. Patrick's Day is celebrated in many parts of the world, and suggested that she look up the history of the holiday in the encyclopedia. Ophelia said she couldn't because that volume of the encyclopedia was missing from the book case. She thought maybe it had been lost when they moved from their old apartment last summer.

"I really don't think you're looking on the right shelf," said her mother. "I saw that volume last week."

"I don't have time to look for it now," called Ophelia. "I need to go to the store to get a present for Pat. I think he'd like a kite."

"That sounds like a good idea," her mother replied. "March is such a windy month that he will surely be able to fly it!"

List 6 facts from Ophelia's story.

1. _____
2. _____
3. _____
4. _____
5. _____
6. _____

List 6 opinions from Ophelia's story.

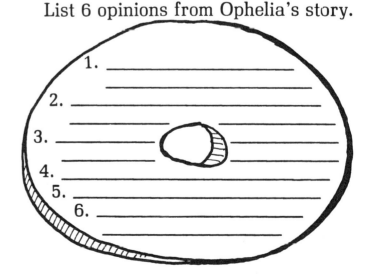

1. _____
2. _____
3. _____
4. _____
5. _____
6. _____

GET THE POINT!

Distinguishing facts from opinions is not always easy. This is especially true in advertising. A producer thinks that his product is a good one, and wants you to buy it, so the product is described in terms that will make you think good thoughts about it and convince you that you need it.

Read the magazine ad below. Underline the facts in red and the opinions in blue. Be careful—sometimes they are mixed together in the same sentence!

PENCIL PACKERS, INC. presents . . .

THE POINT.

. . . the *BEST* and most *MARVELOUS* PENCIL SHARPENER to ever appear on the market!!!

This powerful new pencil sharpener needs no plugs, no cords, no electrical outlets. It is battery-powered, and we think it will run for at least 3 years on its original units. Constructed with solid, top-quality aluminum blades, this machine will give your pencils sharper, cleaner, finer points than any produced by our competitors. There's no waiting, no messy dust or pencil shavings, no energy output on your part! Simply drop your pencil into the machine, and watch it roll out with the best point a pencil could have . . .

FAST, FAST, FAST!!!!!

You need this wonderful, work-saving tool—

. . . *at home* . . . *at the office*

. . . *at school* . . . *ANYWHERE you need a pencil!*

So hurry to your local *PENCIL PACKERS* dealer, and buy this remarkable sharpener at the special introductory bargain price of only $9.95. Supplies are limited, so don't delay!!

Get . . .

THE POINT.

Remember . . . at *PENCIL PACKERS, INC.*, serving YOU is a *POINT* of PRIDE!

Rewrite this ad using only the facts. Then write a short paragraph explaining which opinions in the original ad interested you, and tell why.

REASONING CAN BE PUZZLING!

PURPOSE: Determining cause and effect

PREPARATION

1. Gather the following materials.
   - —24 construction paper squares or 3″ x 5″ index cards
   - —felt pens
   - —box with top

2. Print two sentences (one cause, one effect) on each of the cards.

3. Cut each card into two uneven puzzle pieces. Make sure one whole sentence remains on each half. (Think about design as you print the cards.)

PROCEDURE

1. Place all the cards on the table before you.

2. Match cause and effect sentences. You will know when you have a correct match because the pieces will fit together perfectly.

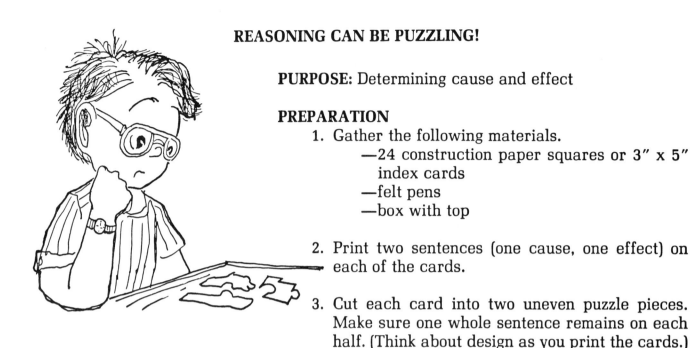

144

JUST BECAUSE

The pictures in eight of these circles show something that happened. Each picture in the other eight shows an effect of one of the happenings. Draw lines to connect each "cause" circle with the correct "effect" circle.

CAUSES

EFFECTS

Select one "cause" and "effect" circle set to use as the theme for a creative story.

MOOD MINDED

Below are several story excerpts in which the author's purpose was to create a definite mood or feeling. Read each one carefully, and identify its mood or feeling by matching each excerpt with a picture that shows the same mood. Draw an arrow from the excerpt to the picture.

Then reread each story, and underline the key words that helped you to know what the mood of the story was. (Excerpt A is done for you.)

A. The house stood **still** and **gaunt**— a **stark** silhouette against the **dull gray** sky, framed only by two **spindly** pines and a **lone, wind-whipped** Joshua tree.

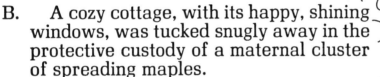

B. A cozy cottage, with its happy, shining windows, was tucked snugly away in the protective custody of a maternal cluster of spreading maples.

C. Above, the clouds, lighted silver by a full moon, shaded the shimmering beauty of the crystal-like waters below.

D. Jessica awoke, instantly alert and full of spirit. She climbed quickly from her lofty bunk with a nimble animation that resembled the early-morning activities of the jays and squirrels outside her window. She was exuberantly delighted to be alive.

With Pen in Hand

PURPOSE: Identification with fictional characters

PREPARATION

1. Provide dual copies of paperback books, or reproduce two copies of a story or an excerpt so that two students have the identical material. Selection should be based on a well-developed character portrait of two or more interacting characters, like those found in the following.

   Sleeping Beauty — Sleeping Beauty and the Good Fairy
   Hansel and Gretel — Gretel and the Step-mother
   Cinderella — Cinderella and the oldest step-sister
   The Adventures of Robin Hood — Robin Hood and Maid Marion
   Winnie the Pooh — Piglet and Pooh
   Little Women — Jo and Beth
   Madeline — Madeline and Miss Clavel

PROCEDURE

1. Working in pairs, students read the selected material. Then each chooses one of the two main characters to represent.

2. Each student writes a letter from the story character he/she represents to the other story character expressing a personal view of some particular topic or event in the story with implications for the other and/or for common acquaintances.

3. Letters are put in envelopes, addressed and exchanged. Without any discussion, the letters are read and answered.

4. After the answering letters are exchanged and read, the two letter writers sit down to verbally share the viewpoints expressed, and to discuss any conflicts of opinion or perception caused by each character's position.

TINKER BELLE

PLOT A CHARACTERIZATION

PURPOSE: Identifying character traits

PREPARATION

1. Reproduce the "Plot a Characterization" work sheet.

2. Guide each student in selecting a book that portrays one person's life and/or times. Biographies and autobiographies are natural choices, but other selections may be appropriate for special student needs, and fiction may be of more interest in some situations.

PROCEDURE

1. Follow the directions on the "Plot a Characterization" work sheet.

2. Display copies of completed worksheets for discussion.

PLOT A CHARACTERIZATION

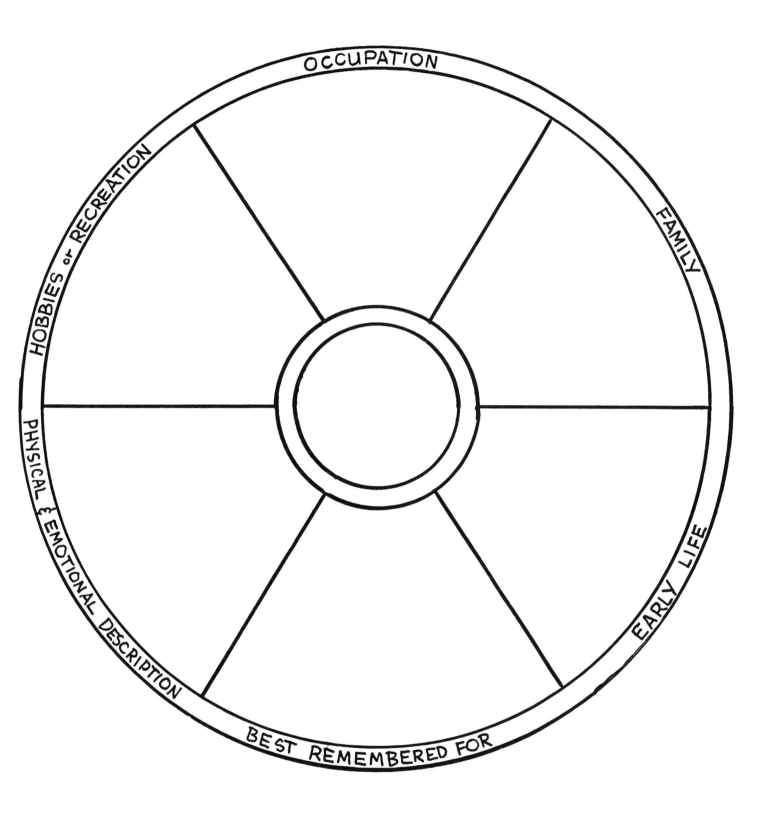

Write events, words, phrases, descriptive sentences or other information about the person being characterized in each spoke of the wheel. Then fill the center circle with words that describe the person's character.

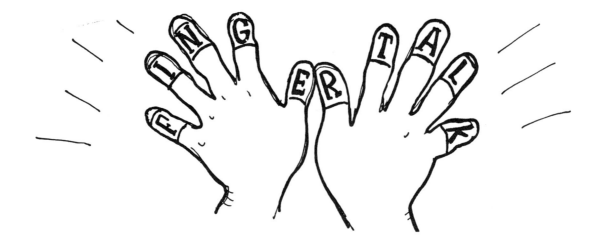

Select any three to six puppets on the following page to be characters in a play. Color and cut out the puppets, and tape the rings together to fit your fingers.

Write the dialogue for a play in which the puppets you have chosen will "act." Give your players very strong character traits to make the play more interesting. Practice your play, and present it to the class.

FINGER TALK

STORIES TO BUILD

PURPOSE: Sensitivity to plot and sequence

PREPARATION

1. Reproduce the stories on the following page. Cut the sentences apart, and place them in large envelopes.

2. Add paper and pencils for student use.

3. Make the complete stories available to students for self-checking.

4. Write the following directions on the front of each envelope.

PROCEDURE

1. Take all of the sentences out of the envelope and spread them out before you.

2. Read each one carefully. Then build the story by arranging the sentences in the correct sequence.

3. After you have arranged the sentences to tell the story, use the paper and pencil to write an ending for the story. Remember to build plot and sequence, and make your ending as exciting as possible.

4. Sign your name as author and put it in the envelope for others to read.

STORIES TO BUILD

An Underground Adventure

Tom and Jerry are good friends.

They play together almost every day.

Three of their favorite games are "wood tag," "kick the can" and "I spy."

One day, they were playing in a vacant lot when they saw a big hole in the ground.

As they looked more closely at the hole, they discovered that it was actually the opening to a big, underground tunnel.

Naturally, they decided to crawl into the hole and do a bit of underground exploring.

Tom crawled in slowly, and Jerry was right behind him.

A Trip to the Zoo

The boys and girls in Mr. Jones' fifth grade class could hardly believe that the big day had finally arrived.

For weeks, they had been planning for their trip to the zoo.

As they climbed onto the big, yellow bus for the fifteen-mile ride, they were filled with excitement and expectations.

The bus driver discussed rules, and Mr. Jones gave each student a map and a booklet about the animals in the zoo.

Just as the driver called, "Let's go," and started the motor, Mrs. Goodlady, the principal, came to the door of the school and yelled, "Stop! Stop where you are!"

CARTOON CAPERS

PURPOSE: Visualizing

PREPARATION

1. Cut ten cartoons with captions from newspapers or magazines.

2. Cut the cartoons and captions apart.

3. Number each cartoon and its corresponding caption.

4. Place cartoons in one envelope and captions in another.

5. Copy the Procedure directions, and place them with the envelopes.

PROCEDURE

1. Number your paper from 1 to 20.

2. Take **only** the cartoons from the envelope.

3. Begin with cartoon number 1. Study it carefully, and write an appropriate caption.

4. Continue until you have done all 20.

5. Remove the original captions from the other envelope.

6. Check and compare your cartoon captions with the original ones.

MORE CARTOON CAPERS

PURPOSE: Visualizing

PREPARATION

1. Cut topics from newspapers or magazines, or write titles appropriate for cartoon captions on strips of paper.

2. Place the captions in a basket with a handle or in a plastic pail. Add paper and felt pens.

3. Place the basket or pail and a loose-leaf notebook in a free choice interest center, and print the following directions on a study guide.

PROCEDURE

1. Select a cartoon caption.

2. Use a sheet of paper and pens from the basket to illustrate the caption.

3. Sign your cartoon, and add it to the "Cartoon Capers" notebook.

155

I'D RATHER SEE ONE THAN BE ONE!

Read the following paragraph carefully. Then (not before, please) read and follow the directions given after the paragraph.

The hippodoraffe is native to cool, dry climates; is a vegetarian, and is often spotted near tall fruit or berry-producing trees or shrubs. All evidence indicates that the extra long neck and large stomach pouch make it possible for a hippodoraffe to store and maintain up to a week's supply of food and water in its own body. This enables the animal to use its long legs and big feet to the best advantage to take giant strides, run fast and cover many miles in any given day. For this reason, a hippodoraffe is seldom victim to hunters or other enemies, and usually enjoys a long and healthy life span. Hippodoraffes are reported to be strong and cunning, and yet very gentle and cooperative. This evidence, as is all other data about the hippodoraffe's life style and characteristics, is poorly documented due to the limited number available for observation. Scientists are continually on the lookout for a way to secure one or more pairs to place in captivity for observation purposes.

Draw a picture of the hippodoraffe in its natural environment. Color your picture.

Hippodoraffe

Reread the paragraph, and underline the three sentences that caused you to visualize the hippodoraffe as you did.

COMPREHENSION SKILLS COMPETENCY REVIEW

Read this news bulletin carefully.

News Bulletin

Just after noon today, three prisoners escaped from the State Prison located at 4609 Cumberland Circle East. These three prisoners are thought to be armed, and are considered very dangerous. At the time of their escape, they were wearing olive green prison uniforms. They escaped by hooking bed sheets together to make a rope to scale the prison wall. All three were serving 99-year sentences for murder and armed robbery. They are from the western part of the state, and have each served 13 years of their sentences. The prisoners are thought to be on foot, still together and seeking a way to get out of the state. Police helicopters joined in the search about two hours after the escape. All area residents are asked to be on the alert for these escaped prisoners, and to call local police at this number, 876-5429, if they have any reason to think they have spotted these people.

1. Draw a straight line under the three sentences in the News Bulletin containing information that would be important for area residents to remember.

2. Draw a circle around the sentence that tells how the prisoners escaped.

3. Put parentheses around the sentence that gives the main idea of the News Bulletin.

4. Make a box around the four words that describe the escaped prisoners' clothes.

5. Draw a circle around the phrase that does not tell about the escaped prisoners.

> . . . considered very dangerous . . .
> . . . wearing olive green prison uniforms . . .
> . . . police helicopters joined the search . . .

6. Draw a circle around the sentence that tells what happened first.

> The prisoners are thought to be seeking a way to get out of the state.
> Just after noon today, three prisoners escaped from the State Prison.
> Police helicopters joined in the search about two hours after the escape.

7. Write the three sentences that would best summarize the News Bulletin.

_____
_____
_____
_____
_____
_____

8. Circle the phrase that tells that the prisoners have been in prison for more than ten years.

> All three were serving 99-year sentences for murder and armed robbery. They are from the western part of the state, and have served 13 years of their sentences.

9. Draw a circle around the word that best completes this sentence.

   A driver is to a bus as a pilot is to _____.

   > a movie theater
   > an airplane
   > a farm

10. Draw a circle around the phrase that best describes what the children are most apt to do.

    A clap of thunder followed the lightning. The children

    > . . . gathered their things and ran for shelter.
    > . . . spread their picnic lunch on the sand.
    > . . . decided to go swimming.

11. Draw a circle around the phrase that tells what would be most apt to happen.

    As the house seemed to explode into flames, the

    > . . . children ran closer.
    > . . . children began to sing and dance.
    > . . . children screamed for help.

12. Draw a line through the sentence that does not belong.

    Yesterday I went to the library to find a book of fairy tales. There was one by Hans Christian Andersen, and there was one called *The Blue Book of Fairy Tales*. My mother said we were going to have hamburgers for dinner.

13. Draw a line through the sentence that is an opinion rather than a fact.

    For centuries, soldiers have gone into battle. Many have lost their lives. All soldiers are strong and brave.

14. Underline the three words that portray the mood of the sentence.

    The house stood still and gaunt, a stark silhouette against the gray sky.

15. Draw a circle around the phrase that describes the actor's character.

    The surly and selfish egocentric actor was dressed in his costume and ready to go on stage.

16. Number these sentences as they would appear in a story.

    __ Tom crawled in slowly, and Jerry followed.
    __ Tom and Jerry saw a big hole in the ground.
    __ They decided to crawl into the hole.

CLUBHOUSE

BE KIND TO BEAVERS ...

SKILLSTUFF

Reading Study Skills

IV. READING STUDY SKILLS

____ Can use the dictionary

    ____ alphabetize

    ____ use guide words, symbols and keys

____ Can determine what reference source to use and use multiple resources related to one topic

    ____ thesaurus and encyclopedia

    ____ library materials

    ____ catalogs, magazines and newspapers

    ____ table of contents, index and glossary

____ Can read and use systematically organized materials

    ____ maps and globes

    ____ charts, tables, graphs and diagrams

____ Can understand and use punctuation

____ Can follow written directions

____ Can outline material read

____ Can take notes from reading

____ Can skim to locate facts and details

____ Can organize facts to support a conclusion

____ Is developing increased reading rate, accuracy and independence

OOMPAH!

PURPOSE: Functional dictionary usage

PREPARATION

1. Gather the following materials.
   —5″ × 7″ index cards
   —red and blue felt pens
   —dictionaries
   —dark-colored crayons or
     washable felt pens
   —safety pins

2. Write each of the following word sets in red on one set of index cards. Make a duplicate set of cards in blue.

```
l _ _ _              _ _ _ k            _ _ _ _ r
m _ _ _ _ _          _ _ _ t  h         g _ _ _
_ _ m                w _ _ _            s  t _ _ _ _
_ _ _ _ _ s          q _ _ _ _          v _ _ _
_ _ _ l  e           _ _ e _            t _ _
b  r _ _ _ _         _ _ o _            _ n _ _ _
_ a _ _                                 _ _ _ _ e  s
```

3. Divide the class into two teams. Pin red cards on the shirts of one team; pin blue cards on the shirts of the other team.

4. Provide dictionaries and dark-colored crayons or washable felt pens for each student.

5. Give the "Go" signal.

PROCEDURE

1. Each student looks through a dictionary to find a word that will fit the spaces and letters designated on his/her card.

2. When a student finds a word, he/she asks a teammate to write the word on the card.

3. When all team members have words written correctly on their cards, they line up in alphabetical order and call out in unison, "Oompah!"

4. The first team to do this receives 5 points. Each team also receives 5 points for each correct word in alphabetical order. One point is deducted for each misspelling or for each word out of alphabetical order.

5. Points are totaled, and the team with the highest score wins.

LETTERED LUNCHES

The children at Andover school have trouble finding their own lunch boxes. Help them by cutting out the lunch boxes below and pasting each one in its alphabetically assigned space on the shelves.

LETTERED LUNCHES

OOPS! WRONG PAGE!

Cross out the words that do not belong on each dictionary page. Use the guide words to help you.

cow **cut**

come   cub
crab   chair
creek   curl
crow   curly
crown   cut

leg **live**

lemon   limp
let   lap
lie   line
light   list
laugh   love

Dictionary
New Land Dictionary
Old World DICTIONARY

men **mouse**

mess   miss
milk   mix
mad   meat
mat   mop
mile   mother

pat **puppy**

paw   pizza
pen   plane
pet   dog
pick   play
bat   pool

seal **soon** **hello** **hurry**

see   sick   hen   hog
set   sat   hide hop
shark sister he   hot
chip sleep hill hug
ship snake hat hurt

eraser

My Pencil

WATCH OUT, WEBSTER!

PURPOSE: Using phonetic symbols and keys.

PREPARATION
1. Provide the following materials.
   —paper
   —pencils, pens and/or crayons
   —dictionaries

2. Ask each student to choose a subject of special interest to him/her, and create a "mini-dictionary" containing only words associated with that topic.

Examples:

The Dog Dictionary	The Dictionary of Music
Words about Airplanes	The Shell Dictionary
	People Words

Each mini-dictionary should contain from 10-25 words, depending upon the capabilities of the student.

PROCEDURE
1. Students prepare their pages carefully, giving appropriate words, the proper pronunciation key for each, a strong definition and, if possible, an illustration. Students then make their finished pages into booklets.

2. Each student presents his/her finished dictionary to the class by sharing at least 3 entries from it with classmates.

DISCONCERTING DICTIONARIES

PURPOSE: Using dictionary skills/interpreting symbols and keys

PREPARATION

1. Provide assorted colors of construction paper and felt pens for student use. Have several dictionaries on hand for students to use as references.

2. Write the directions below on a card, and place it with the other materials in a free-choice interest center.

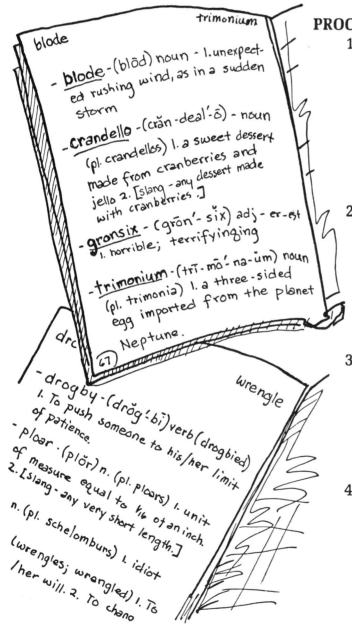

PROCEDURE

1. Create 20 nonsense words to go into a "No-Such-Word" Dictionary, and decide what part of speech each word is. Browse through a dictionary to see how information like plurals and endings is shown, and use that format as a guide to show all the "technical" information you have created for each of your words.

2. Write 4 or 5 words (in alphabetical order, of course) with the accompanying "technical information" (phonetic symbols and keys) on sheets of construction paper. Leave room to add definitions and illustrations later. Make an attractive cover, sign your name as "1st Author" and clip your pages together.

3. Exchange your "No-Such-Word" Dictionary for one written by a classmate. Read and think about his/her words. Then fill in a definition for each word, and write a sentence for each that shows your interpretation of the meaning you have given it.

4. Sign your name as "2nd Author," and discuss both completed "No-Such-Word" Dictionaries with your co-author.

166

RELEVANT REFERENCES

Work the crossword puzzle below to show off your knowledge of sources that are used to locate information.

Where would you look to:

ACROSS

2. Check the day of the month?
6. Find a phone number?
9. Locate a library book?
10. Determine the distance between two cities?
11. Find information about the life and habits of elephants?

DOWN

1. Get ideas about fashion and/or home decorating?
3. Find the time of a favorite TV program and local advertising?
4. Learn where the world's deserts are located?
5. Find how many teaspoons equal one cup?
6. Find synonyms for a word?
7. Find the definition of a word?
8. Find the cost of a bicycle?

QUESTIONS TO ANSWER

PURPOSE: Using reference materials to find answers to specific questions

PREPARATION

1. Provide the following materials for the students.
   —question mark cards
   —box
   —atlas, encyclopedia, almanac, dictionary, thesaurus, *Guiness Book of World Records*, etc.
   —pencils or pens
   —paper

2. Use this pattern or one of your own to make question marks.

3. Print one of the statements or questions from the following page (or use some of your own) on each question mark. Print a number on the back.

4. Print the following directions in the top of the flat box, and place the question marks in the box for student use.

PROCEDURE

1. Select a question mark from the box. Read it carefully, and decide which reference books to use to find the best answer in the shortest time.

2. When you have located the information, write the number from the back of the question mark on your paper, the reference book used, the page number and how long it took you to locate the information.

3. Finish as many of the question mark questions as you can in the time you have assigned.

QUESTIONS TO ANSWER

1. What is the difference between a souffle and an omelet?

2. Name six words that mean the same thing as "desert country."

3. In what countries would you find a Shah, a king and a prime minister?

4. What is a polygraph?

5. What is the most heavily populated country in the world?

6. Where and when was the first airplane flown?

7. Name three sources to use to locate information about filmmaking.

8. What is a palindrome, and in what subjects in school would you need this definition?

9. Who was Copernicus, and what were his contributions to mankind?

10. What is the world land speed record?

11. What was Harriet Tubman known for?

12. Who compiled the first dictionary, and how long did it take?

13. Who was Alfred Nobel?

14. Who was the first woman astronaut?

TOWERING THESAURUS

PURPOSE: Using the thesaurus.

PREPARATION

1. Print appropriate category words on each shape on the "Towering Thesaurus" work sheet.

2. Reproduce the "Towering Thesaurus" work sheet.

3. Provide a thesaurus and the following Procedure directions for each participating student.

PROCEDURE

1. Use a thesaurus to find words associated with each category word given. Write the words you found in the appropriate blocks. (At least ten words must be listed in a shape before it may be used as a building block.)

2. When all the shapes have been filled, cut them out and paste them on another sheet of paper to build your own Thesaurus Tower.

3. Use your crayons to decorate and add interest to the completed tower.

PURPOSE: Using the encyclopedia

PREPARATION

1. Lead a group discussion of the encyclopedia and its uses. Ask students to identify the volume to use to locate information related to various topics, emphasizing that information can be found in more than one volume, but that there is usually one which has more comprehensive coverage. This volume, then, is the primary source of information on the topic.

2. Provide encyclopedias and copies of the "High Flying Flags" work sheet.

PROCEDURE

1. Complete the work sheet as directed.

FOLLOW-UP ACTIVITY

1. Divide students into small groups to research countries represented by the flags.

2. Each group selects or is assigned a different country, and uses the encyclopedia to learn as much as possible about the geography, history, customs, industry and social life of the country and its people.

3. At an appointed time, the groups will share their findings through any creative means they choose. Some suggestions are: a panel discussion, mural, puppet or stage play, diorama or scrapbook.

HIGH FLYING FLAGS

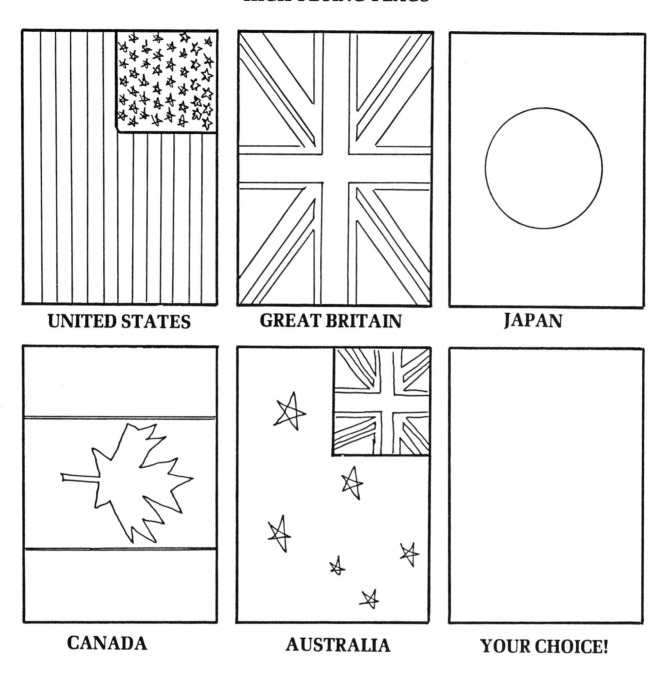

UNITED STATES   GREAT BRITAIN   JAPAN

CANADA   AUSTRALIA   YOUR CHOICE!

1. Use the encyclopedia to find out what crayons to use to color each of the above flags. Then color the flags correctly.

2. Write the volume and page number (or numbers) on which the information was found.

   Volume: _____   Page: _____

3. Thumb through this volume to find other information about flags. Write a short paragraph summarizing this information.

   _____
   _____
   _____
   _____

MAIL-ORDER MADNESS

PURPOSE: Using catalogs.

PREPARATION

1. Provide several mail-order catalogs from your own supply, and ask students to bring some from home.

2. Produce copies of the "Mail-Order Madness" work sheet, and provide paper and pencils for the students.

3. Write the following introduction to the activity on a sheet of paper.

Mail-Order Madness

Now that more and more people are working and have less leisure time to do their shopping, it seems that "Mail-Order Madness" is here to stay. All kinds of companies send their catalogs through the mail to convince the customer to buy books, records, clothing, accessories, toys, cards and even flower seeds "at home" by filling out an enclosed order blank and sending it, along with a check, back to the company.

There are many good things about shopping by mail. One is the convenience of doing your shopping at home. This appeals to lots of people, especially during holiday seasons when stores are crowded and stock has been "picked over." It also helps people who can't leave home because of illness or a disability of some sort.

A careful consumer must know how to read a catalog, find prices, notice hidden costs and add charges correctly. The customer must also be aware that pictures and explanations of items are provided by the company, and be able to see past the glowing descriptions to understand what the item really is or does.

4. Place all materials, including the directions below, in a free-choice interest center for individual student use.

PROCEDURE

1. Read the "Mail-Order Madness" introduction sheet.

2. Choose a catalog from the ones provided, and answer the "Mail-Order Madness" work sheet questions on a separate piece of paper.

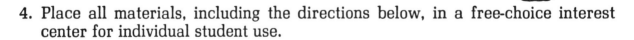

1. What company sent out the catalog you are using? Where is it located?

2. Was the catalog sent to a particular person, or is it marked "Occupant"? How do you suppose that companies get the names and addresses of the people to whom they send catalogs? List at least two ways.

3. Does your catalog have a Table of Contents or an Index? If so, how do these help you? If not, tell whether or not you think they are necessary and why.

4. Is the catalog broken down into sections or divisions? If so, how does that help you, and what are the divisions? If not, list the divisions **you** would have made, and tell why.

5. Do the catalog items have order numbers? Why or why not?

6. How do you figure out how much an item costs?

7. Are there any coupons for free gifts, or any "incentives" that make you want to order more items than you had planned? How do these "freebies" help the company?

8. Are mailing costs, taxes and other charges listed clearly in the catalog? What do these extra charges do to your cost?

9. How long will you have to wait before you receive your order? Does waiting made a difference to you? Why?

Special Order Coupon

Choose 5 items from the catalog that you'd like to have. Fill out the order blank, being sure to include all information needed (name of item, number, color, size, etc.). Write your name and address clearly on the form so the company will know exactly where to send your order. Add shipping charges, taxes and other costs (if any) to the cost of your items, and total your order.

Then find out how much it would cost you to buy the same items at a store in your town. Figure the difference between the two. Which shopping method will cost more money? Which is more important to you in this case, money or convenience? Why?

Card Catalog Cogitation

The card catalog in every library has cards listing each book three ways: by subject, title and author. If you know any of these 3 facts about a book, you can find a listing for it in the card catalog.

Read each statement below. If the statement is true, color in the corresponding number blocks in the picture.

1. If you wanted to read all the "Just So" stories by Rudyard Kipling, you would first look in the card catalog for an author card with his name.
2. If you wanted to find out about the history of the United Nations, you would first look for a title card.
3. If you wanted to write an article about the world hunger crisis, you would first look for a subject card.
4. If you wanted to know who wrote *Mary Poppins*, you would look first for an author card.
5. If you wanted to make a list of all the books written by Charles Dickens, you would look first for a title card.
6. If you wanted to find a copy of *Spoon River Anthology*, you would first look for a title card.
7. If you wanted to read some of Eldridge Cleaver's writing, you would look first for a subject card.
8. If you wanted to know who wrote *Bambi*, you would look first for a title card.
9. If you remembered that Nikki Giovanni wrote a book of poetry that you wanted to read, but you couldn't remember the title of it, you would look first for an author card.
10. If you wanted to find J.R.R. Tolkein's book about hobbits, you would first find the title card.
11. If you wanted to browse through a collection of fairy tales by Jakob and Wilhelm Grimm, you would first look for an author card.
12. If you wanted to read Kenneth Grahame's book about the wild animals living along the river bank, you would first look for a title card.
13. If you wanted to find out more about scouting, you would first look for a title card.

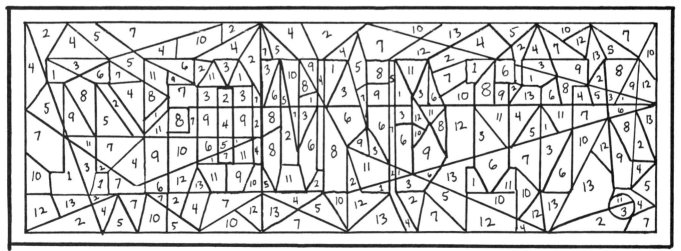

WORD ROUND - UP

PURPOSE: Using newspapers and magazines.

PREPARATION

1. Use the weekly classroom newspapers or magazines to teach or reinforce word attack or vocabulary skills. Provide a copy of the paper or magazine, along with paper and pencils or pens, for each student.

2. Choose one or more of the following activities for the students, and direct them to find and circle or list all words that fit into that category.

—words with a given beginning or ending sound

—words containing a specific blend or vowel sound

—words containing a vowel sound controlled by "R"

—four-, five-, six- or seven-letter words

—words with a specified number of syllables

—homonyms, antonyms, synonyms or heteronyms

—words with double letters

—words with prefixes or suffixes

—contractions

—compound words

—plurals

—possessives

—words rhyming with a word printed on the chalkboard

ADAPTATION

To provide variety, all the above activities and others appropriate to group needs may be printed on cards which are placed in a basket to be passed around so that each student may select one card.

CONTEMPLATING THE CONTENTS

PURPOSE: Using the Table of Contents

PREPARATION

1. Choose a book of common interest to students that contains a Table of Contents (example: *The Wind in the Willows*).

2. Go through the book, and choose one word from each consecutive chapter to put together to make a message for the students. Be sure that the words you have chosen will fit together in the order the students find them to form a sensible sentence.

Chart Format

Chapter Title	Page #	Para-graph #	Sen-tence #	Word #	Word

3. Make a chart like the one above using the book of your choice. Leave the "Chapter Title" and "Word" columns blank.

4. Place the book, the chart, some paper and pencils along with the following directions in a free-choice activity center for individual student use.

PROCEDURE

1. Divide your paper into two columns.

2. In the first column, fill in each chaper title in the order in which it appears in the book.

CONTEMPLATING THE CONTENTS

3. Follow the directions on the chart to find the message words. Fill in each word from a chapter beside the chapter title. (Note to the teacher: do the first line for your students if desired.)

4. Write your completed sentence across the bottom of the page.

5. Illustrate your paper with characters and scenes from the book.

Sample Chart using *The Wind in the Willows*

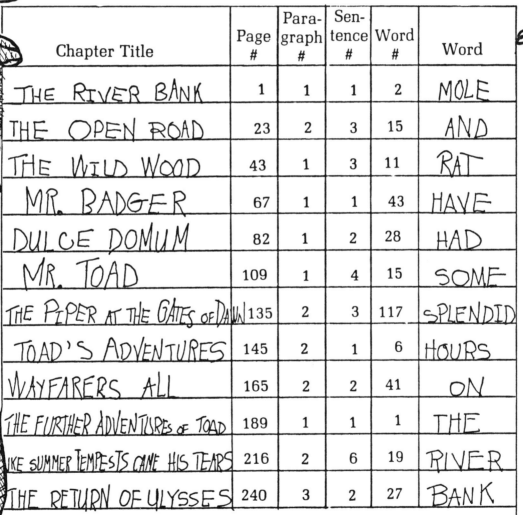

Chapter Title	Page #	Paragraph #	Sentence #	Word #	Word
THE RIVER BANK	1	1	1	2	MOLE
THE OPEN ROAD	23	2	3	15	AND
THE WILD WOOD	43	1	3	11	RAT
MR. BADGER	67	1	1	43	HAVE
DULCE DOMUM	82	1	2	28	HAD
MR. TOAD	109	1	4	15	SOME
THE PIPER AT THE GATES OF DAWN	135	2	3	117	SPLENDID
TOAD'S ADVENTURES	145	2	1	6	HOURS
WAYFARERS ALL	165	2	2	41	ON
THE FURTHER ADVENTURES OF TOAD	189	1	1	1	THE
IKE SUMMER TEMPESTS CAME HIS TEARS	216	2	6	19	RIVER
THE RETURN OF ULYSSES	240	3	2	27	BANK

Completed Sentence: MOLE AND RAT HAVE HAD SOME SPLENDID HOURS ON THE RIVER BANK.

179

AN INDEX INDICATES

An index is a listing of terms and subject areas which can be found in the back of some books. It is presented in alphabetical order, and the page number on which each item appears is also given. This tool helps a reader who knows what information he/she is looking for, but cannot find it from the Table of Contents.

Many school books, like history and science texts, contain indexes. Other books, like poetry anthologies and biographies, also have them. Find several books which have indexes, and study these until you understand index form.

Choose at least 11 of your favorite poems, and copy each on a separate sheet of paper. (Hint: cut regular sheets of paper into halves or quarters, and write one poem on each side of a page.) Number your pages, and make a cover (with the title of your choice) and a Table of Contents for your book.

Then index your poems according to **subject matter,** like this:

or **authors' names,** like this:

or even by a **listing of the first line of each poem,** like this:

Remember to put your entries in alphabetical order, and list the correct page number beside each. Write your index on the last page of your book, add a back cover and staple or bind your pages together.

Glancing At The GLOSSARY

PURPOSE: Using the glossary

PREPARATION:

1. Choose a classroom text with a glossary. Be certain each student has a copy of the text.

2. Divide the class into two teams.

3. Make chalk and a section of the chalkboard available for the game.

PROCEDURE

1. The teacher calls out a word from the glossary.

2. The first student on each team looks through the glossary to find the word, runs to the chalkboard and writes the word and its definition on the board. The first student to complete the writing receives one point for his/her team.

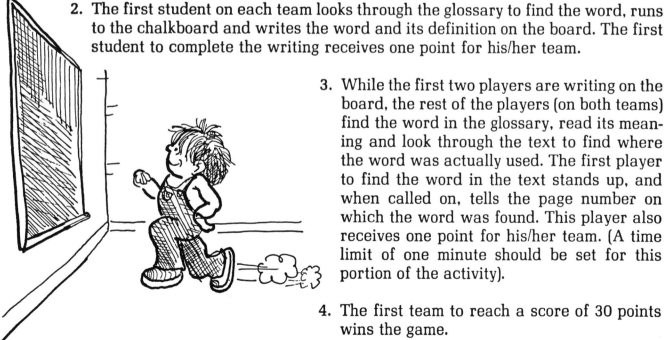

3. While the first two players are writing on the board, the rest of the players (on both teams) find the word in the glossary, read its meaning and look through the text to find where the word was actually used. The first player to find the word in the text stands up, and when called on, tells the page number on which the word was found. This player also receives one point for his/her team. (A time limit of one minute should be set for this portion of the activity).

4. The first team to reach a score of 30 points wins the game.

PIN A PLACE

PURPOSE: Using a map to check known facts

PREPARATION

1. Gather the following materials.
   - —large map of your community
   - —red or yellow yarn
   - —straight pins
   - —paper
   - —scissors
   - —colored felt pens

2. Place the large map of your city or community on a bulletin board easily accessible to the students.

3. Draw a fat red circle around the location of your school. Cut out a tiny paper school building, and print the name of your school on it. Pin the symbol inside the circle.

4. Cut paper into strips, and pin them on the bulletin board by the map.

5. Reproduce the "Pin a Place" work sheet, and place it with the straight pins, yarn and pens by the bulletin board.

PIN A PLACE

1. Find your street on the map.

2. String a piece of yarn from your street to the school, and from your street to the side of the bulletin board where the sentence strips are pinned.

3. Figure out how far it is from your home to the school. Write your name and the distance on a sentence strip. Attach the end of your piece of yarn to the strip.

4. As you have time, find:

   —your best friend's street

   —all the streets between your house and the school

   —the street on which the grocery store your family shops at is located

   —the street on which the post office is located

   —the river nearest to the school

   —the lake closest to your home

   —a park near your home

   —the public library branch nearest your home

   —the fire station closest to your home

   —the street on which your favorite fast food restaurant is located

   —the main street in your town

ALL ABOUT AUSTRALIA

Read about Australia in your encyclopedia or geography book.

Using what you have learned and a map of Australia, complete the following crossword puzzle.

ACROSS

1. The highest mountain in Australia.
3. The state capital of the Northwest Territory.
9. The body of water found off the coast of Cairns.
10. The Australian flag has this many stars.
11. If you were travelling from Adelaide to Sydney, in which direction would you go?
13. The longest river in Australia.
14. An island state of Australia south of Melbourne.
15. Ocean off the western coast of Australia.
16. Largest seaport in western Australia.

DOWN

2. Australian city with the largest population.
4. Opposite of "Old North Wales."
5. Australian state with Brisbane as its capital city.
6. Australia is close to the _____ Pole.
7. The capital city of Australia.
8. A state in Australia named for a famous English queen.
12. Australia is not only a country; it is also a _____.

WORLDLY  WISE

Use your globe to complete these sentences.

1. The largest country in Europe is _____.

2. The country directly north of the United States is _____.

3. _____ is the European country closest to Africa.

4. _____ is the largest Caribbean island.

5. A country which is also a continent is _____.

6. If you are in Nairobi, Kenya, the nearest ocean to you would be _____.

7. The country directly east of Argentina is _____.

8. The large body of water which separates Europe from Africa is _____.

9. The European country which has a shape resembling a boot is _____.

10. North of the Soviet Union, there is a body of water called the _____ Ocean.

11. A large country in Asia of which Peking is the capital city is _____.

12. The country that shares a border with Norway is _____.

AFRICA

SAUDI ARABIA

Plan a trip around the world. Use your globe for help, and write a day-by-day itinerary.

BENJY'S BEST BET

Spring is just around the corner, and Benjy is making plans to buy the mini-bike of his dreams. All winter, he has been saving for the three-horsepower red mini-bike in Mr. Gardner's show window. He has shoveled snow, tended house plants and run errands to earn money, but he still does not have enough.

He has finally decided to borrow the money and work for Mr. Gardner to pay it back. His problem now is to choose the best of these finance plans.

Charge-A-Card Co.
   $40 Down payment; $10.50 monthly payments for 1½ years.
Best Credit Union
   No Down payment; $21.00 monthly payments for 1 year.
Easy Loan Company
   $13.50 Down payment; $13.50 monthly payments for 13 months.
Trusty Bank Loans
   $29.00 Down payment; $29.00 monthly payments for 7 months.

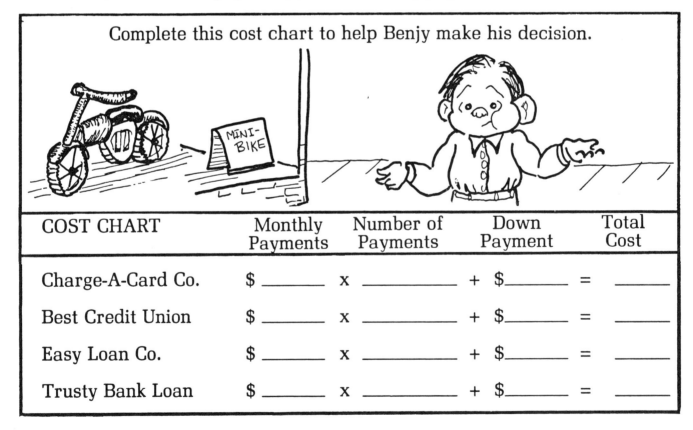

Complete this cost chart to help Benjy make his decision.

COST CHART	Monthly Payments	Number of Payments	Down Payment	Total Cost
Charge-A-Card Co.	$ _____	x _____	+ $_____	= _____
Best Credit Union	$ _____	x _____	+ $_____	= _____
Easy Loan Co.	$ _____	x _____	+ $_____	= _____
Trusty Bank Loan	$ _____	x _____	+ $_____	= _____

Draw a star beside the name of the company offering the best finance plan.

GRAPH GAZING

If you made a graph showing how tall your classmates are, it might look something like this.

TOMMY	39"
STEPHANIE	45"
BETH	43"
JEFF	52"
MIKE	38"
LISA	48"
BOB	42"
MARY	54"
DAVID	41"
JENNIFER	49"

(Graph y-axis: 30 INCHES, 35 INCHES, 40 INCHES, 45 INCHES, 50 INCHES, 55 INCHES)

Using this graph, answer the following questions.

1. Which student is tallest? _____

2. How much taller than David is Stephanie? _____

3. If Tommy were 5 inches taller, how tall would he be? _____

4. Bob wants to be as tall as Mary. How many more inches does he need to grow?_____

5. If the ceiling is 72 inches high, how many more inches could Jeff grow before his head would touch it?_____

6. Lisa is 48 inches tall. How many feet tall is she? _____

7. Which student is the shortest? _____

Use a ruler to measure the heights of six objects in your classroom. Make a graph to show the different heights of the objects. What is the tallest object? What is the shortest one?

187

WILL DR. DOGOOD DO GOOD?

Husky Harry has a weight problem. Dr. Dogood has finally convinced him to follow the famous Dr. Dogood Miracle Diet.

Step #1 on the diet is finding his desired weight. Harry is 4'11" tall. He now weighs 138 pounds.

According to Dr. Dogood's table, he should weigh _____ pounds. This means he needs to lose _____ pounds.

Weight Chart

Height	Male	Female
4'10"	95-105	90-98
4'11"	98-108	93-102
5'	100-111	95-105
5'2"	109-122	98-108
5'4"	118-132	101-112
5'6"	130-143	117-130

This is a fruit and vegetable diet that allows no meat or desserts. Dr. Dogood tells Harry that he should lose 1 pound per day the first, second and third days, and ½ pound each day for the rest of the first week.

On the first day of the second week, Harry is to drink only fruit juices in order to lose two pounds that day. By omitting bread and butter, and eating only two vegetables or one fruit for each meal the rest of the second week, he should lose ½ pound each day.

Fill in this table to show Harry's expected weight loss.

	Day 1	Day 2	Day 3	Day 4	Day 5	Day 6	Day 7
First Week							
Second Week							

If Harry follows the diet plan, he should lose _____ pounds each week.
He will need to diet _____ weeks to reach his desired weight.

188

A PLAIN PAPER PLANE PLAN

Follow this diagram to make a paper airplane.

When you have finished, decorate your airplane in a way that pleases you. Then at recess, have a paper plane race.

PUNCTUATION POINTERS

"Point up" what you know! Work the crossword puzzle to show your knowledge of punctuation skills.

Across

2. When a sentence asks something, a _____ mark goes at the end of it.

3. Use a _____ to separate words in a series.

5. A sentence that shows excitement ends with a(an) _____ mark.

6. Every _____ must have a verb and a subject.

Down

1. A _____ comes at the end of a telling sentence.

2. When you write something down just exactly as someone said it, you put _____ marks around what was said.

4. What comes at the end of an abbreviation like "Mr__"?

CRAYON

Decide which color each punctuation mark makes you think of, and color in the marks. Display your finished page.

LOST IN PUNCTUATION FOREST

Punctuation marks are like trail marks in a forest because they help to guide you through what you read.

Read the story below and supply the missing punctuation. Cross out the punctuation symbols shown here as you place them correctly in the story.

. . . . ! !
¡ ! ! ' ? ' ? ' ? ' ? ( ) ' : ' : ' : ; ; " ; " ; " ; " ; " ; " ; " ; ! " ;
. . .

Sound the alarm cried the principal of G S Evram School Our fourth fifth and sixth grade classes are lost in Punctuation Forest Mr Bledsoe Ms Williams and Mrs Kern their teachers took them there on a fieldtrip to search for the marvelous mysterious morning-blooming Comma Trees that grow hidden deep in the woods and they were to be back no later than 11 00 It's nearly 3 00 now Where can they possibly be

All of the teachers had gathered around they wanted to hear what the principal was saying Ms Alexander the principal sounded very upset so the teachers began to discuss what would be the best thing to do Over their voices Mr Guilford called Listen There are two things to remember in an emergency remain calm and think clearly before you act

Mr Alvarez asked Have the police been notified

Yes replied Ms Alexander they've put out an A P B all points bulletin on them over their radios and the C B people have been contacted too

Well in that case declared Mr Alvarez there's nothing to do but wait

Gloom fell over the group they waited worried and listened in silence Suddenly from far away down the street they heard a loud putt-putt-putt and the creaking sound of a bus coming toward the school Was it could it be Yes It was the missing bus complete with students teachers and driver and armloads of branches from the morning-blooming Comma Trees

Safe at last Ms Alexander sighed with relief as everyone got off the bus Now who is going to explain why you're back so late

Little Books Tell A Lot

PURPOSE: Reading and following written directions

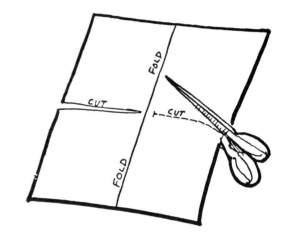

PREPARATION
1. Reproduce the "Little Books Tell a Lot" work sheet.

2. Gather pencils, paper, crayons and/or felt pens for the students.

PROCEDURE
1. Distribute the work sheets.

2. Discuss the assignment with the students, but do not demonstrate how to make the book. (A completed book might be shown to students needing more guidance.)

FOLLOW-UP ACTIVITY
Ask students to select a "Little Book" to review. Arrange a time for book reviews to be presented to the entire group.

LITTLE BOOKS TELL A LOT

1. Fold a sheet of 8½" x 11" white paper down the middle horizontally.

2. Fold the folded sheet vertically to make 4 "pages."

3. Use the scissors to clip through the first fold (almost but not quite all the way across), leaving the paper joined at the center point.

4. Now, you should have a tiny book with 8 pages (counting fronts and backs). Number the pages in the left corners.

5. Select one of the following titles, and write a book about it.

6. Design an attractive cover for the book on page 1. Don't forget to write your own name as author.

7. Write a copyright notice on the inside front cover (page 2). (Use a library book for help if you need it.)

8. On page 3, which is actually the title page of your book, write the title and your name again. Illustrate this page attractively.

9. Plan pages 4, 5, 6 and 7 carefully to tell your entire story. Make it complete and interesting to hold the reader's attention.

10. Design a back cover for page 8.

11. Place your completed book on the reading table to share with your classmates.

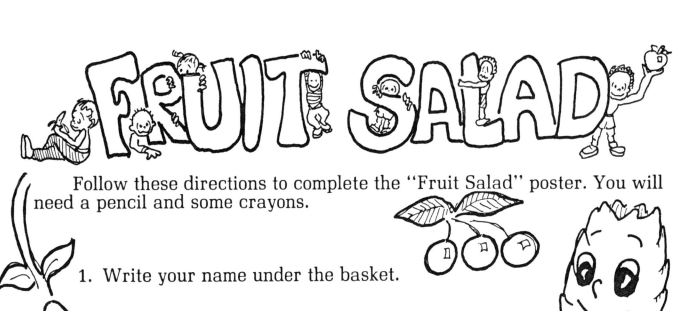

Fruit Salad

Follow these directions to complete the "Fruit Salad" poster. You will need a pencil and some crayons.

1. Write your name under the basket.

2. Draw another leaf on the stem of the apple.

3. Color the apple red, and the stem and leaves green.

4. Write the names of three other fruits that begin with "p" as in "peach."

5. Give the pear a smiling face.

6. Use your pencil to add enough grapes to make an even dozen.

7. Write four words on the banana describing how it would taste.

8. Draw a handle on the basket.

9. Use your favorite color crayon to draw a big bow on the handle.

10. Color all of the fruits.

11. Write a recipe for fruit salad on the basket!

FRUIT SALAD RECIPE:

_____
_____
_____
_____
_____

OUTLINES CAN GO AROUND AND AROUND

PURPOSE: Outlining/organizing ideas

PREPARATION

1. Provide the following materials for the students.
   —outline circles
   —pens
   —paper
   —appropriate books
   —reading or content assignment
      or research projects

2. Reproduce copies of the outline
   circle on the following page.

3. Prepare two or three circles to
   use as examples.

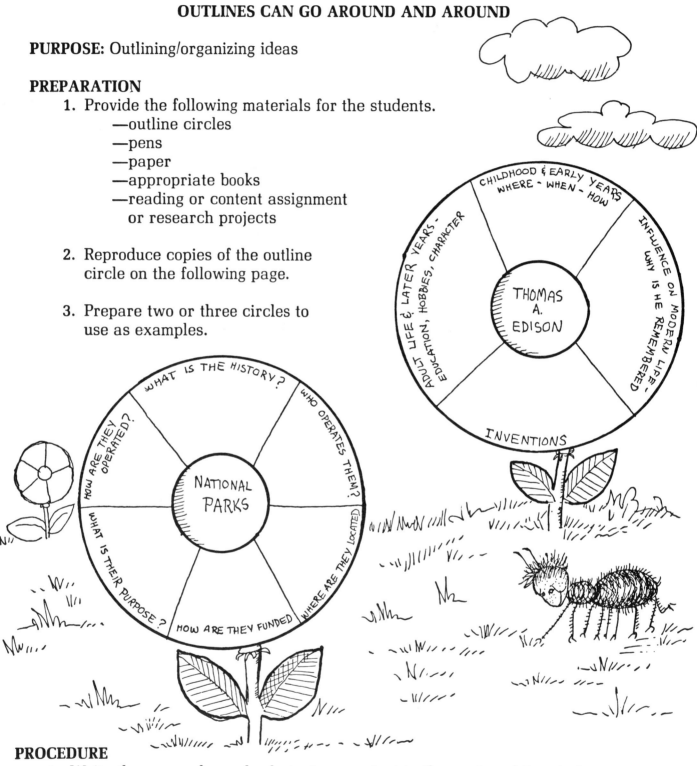

PROCEDURE

1. Write the name of your book, topic or project in the center of the circle.

2. Decide what the main ideas are, and label the circle sections to help you in gathering and organizing your information.

3. Fill each of the sections with the correct information.

CONSIDER THE SOURCE

Discover more about a holiday that interests you by researching the holiday and writing a report of your findings. Use at least three **different** resources (books, magazines, pamphlets, etc.) to learn all you can about its history and development, symbols, traditions, decorations, foods, music and changes in the methods of celebration over the years. Make careful notes, and **then** write your report. **Resources Used:**

1. _____
2. _____
3. _____

Notes

1. Country where holiday originated _____

2. Time _____

3. Purpose or reason for holiday
   _____

4. Customs
   _____
   _____

5. "Things"
   _____
   _____

6. Early celebrations
   _____
   _____

7. Modern-day celebrations
   _____
   _____

8. Other important information
   _____
   _____

Check your notes to be sure you have enough information for an interesting report. If you don't, select a fourth reference book to use.

A QUICK ONCE-OVER

Use a copy of the newspaper to complete this activity.

1. The most important front page news article is about _____ _____ .

2. My horoscope for the day is on page _____ .

3. The name of the main character in the most interesting comic strip in the paper is _____ _____ .

4. A letter to the editor that interested me is about _____ _____

   I (agree/disagree) _____ with the writer's opinion.

5. According to the weather forecast, we should expect tomorrow to be a _____ _____ day.

6. After consulting the TV schedule for this evening, I have found _____ programs that I will probably watch. The one I especially want to see will be shown at _____ o'clock on Channel _____ .

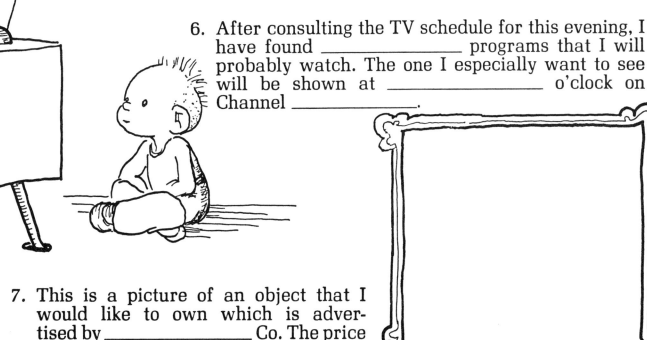

7. This is a picture of an object that I would like to own which is advertised by _____ Co. The price is _____ .

UNDERWATER CHALLENGE

PURPOSE: To organize facts to support a conclusion

PREPARATION

1. Gather the following materials.
   - —large, sturdy corrugated box
   - —scissors or knife
   - —blue and green paper or tempera paint
   - —several different colors of construction paper
   - —glue
   - —thread
   - —felt pens
   - —resource books.

2. Cut one side and half the top from a sturdy corrugated box.

3. Cover the three inside sides of the box with blue paper or paint with blue tempera paint. Cover or paint the outside with green.

4. Provide green, blue, brown, gray, black, white and other colors of construction paper and felt pens. Provide resource books on the ocean and ocean life.

5. Place all materials in a learning center, or allow one reading or study group to take this activity as a "special project."

UNDERWATER CHALLENGE

PROCEDURE

1. Students use resource books to look up plants, animals, shells and/or rocks found under water. They then draw and cut the chosen object from construction paper, label it, write a one-paragraph description of the object and place it beside the diorama.

2. Other students read the paragraphs, sign their names and check (✓) if they think the description is accurate. If they feel it is incorrect or incomplete, they write "I challenge you" beside their name, give three sentences telling why they challenge the report, and giving a resource listing of the book and page number supporting the challenge.

3. If, at the end of the day, the report is unchallenged, the student who originated the object may write his or her name on the paper object and place it in the box. It may be glued to the side, on the bottom or hung by a string from the top to show proper underwater placement.

4. At the end of a given time (usually about a week) the person with the most unchallenged objects placed in the box is declared the "Underwater Expert."

Note: This activity is especially good for academically talented students. They love the "challenge."

AN INSIDE

Think about all the books you have read or hope to read in the near future. Use the card catalog or other resources to help you complete this activity.

1. If I could take only one book on a long journey, I would take _____ because _____ _____.

2. The book I would choose to share with a friend from another country would be _____ because _____ _____.

3. _____ is an author whose books I always enjoy. The thing I like best about books he/she writes is _____ _____.

4. The most beautiful picture book I've ever seen in my whole life is _____. The illustrations are _____ _____.

5. Right now, I am really into reading books about _____ _____.

LOOK AT BOOKS

6. Here is a three-line review of a book I've just read.

   Title of Book: _____

   Review: _____

   _____

   _____.

7. _____ is a book that I

   didn't enjoy. The main thing I disliked about this book was

   _____

   _____.

8. If I had a lot of money to buy books for presents, I would

   buy _____ for my teacher,

   _____ for _____

   _____, and for my own library, I would

   buy _____.

Fasten these two pages together so that the blank sides of the paper form the outsides. Design and color attractive covers, and print the title and your name as author on the front. Use the back cover to list the books you read during the next month.

ON THE LOOKOUT FOR WORDS

Good readers are always on the "lookout" for new words to add to their speaking, reading and writing vocabularies.

As you read this week, add words that you did not know before to this list.

LEARN THE MEANING FOR READING	NEED TO BE ABLE TO SPELL FOR WRITING	LEARN & USE IN CONVERSATION

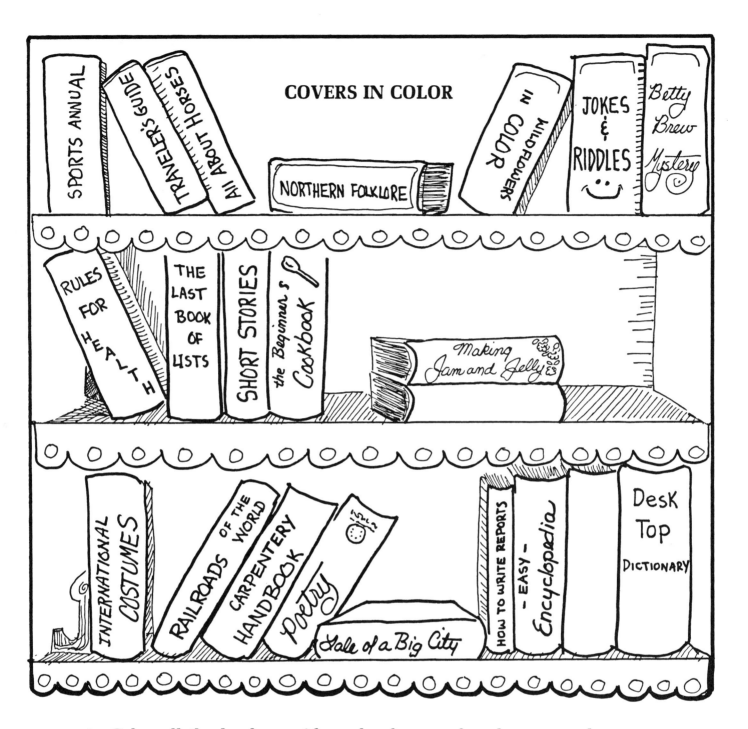

COVERS IN COLOR

1. Color all the books you'd read only once for pleasure red.
2. Make purple stripes on the books you'd use to help you become a better student.
3. Use your blue crayon to decorate the backs of the books you'd look through occasionally for information related to a specific topic.
4. Make green polka dots on the books you'd skim through from time to time but would probably never sit down to read all the way through.
5. Draw gold stars on the books you'd need to read very carefully for important details.
6. Write the names of two special books for your own library shelf on the blank books.

RATE YOUR READING

Even the very best readers can improve their reading skills with a little thought and effort. It's never too early or too late to examine your personal reading habits and take steps to improve them.

In this word-find puzzle, you should be able to locate 27 words related to reading skills. Find and circle each one.

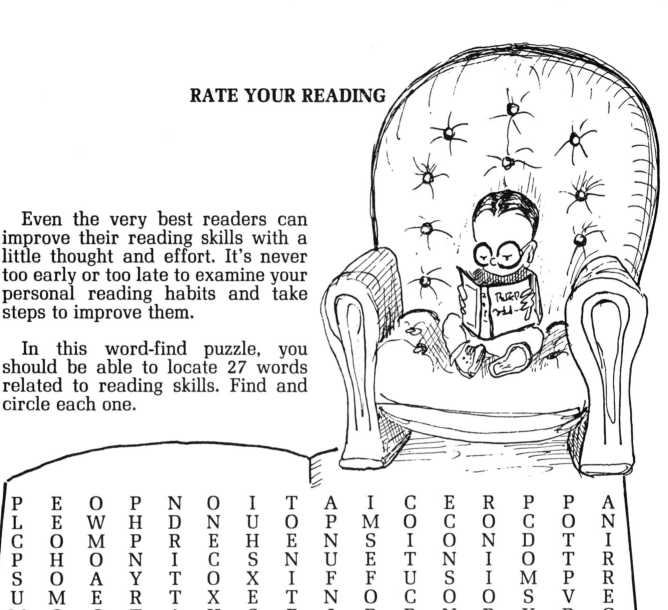

```
P E O P N O I T A I C E R P P A
L E W H D N U O P M O C O N O N
C O M P R E H E N S I O N N D I
P H O N I C S N U E T N I O P R
S O A Y T O X I F F U S O M V R
U M E R T X E T N O C O R S R E
M O C T A H S E I R R N N Y L G
M N N E A C D I L A I A S N G G
A Y E S K I T M I L L N S O N W
R M R A T E I E R E L T D N I L
I G E R O N W A T N N S H Y N E
Z X F P A A N D B I A T D M A E
E I N T R K R E Y R Z A B I E N
V G I C A P C S R L L A T L M S
V O C A B U L A T Y E N D B I I
N L W I M Y N O I N A H T I O E
X I F E R P S W T T T C T R O W
E A S E L C O N   R A     I   N
```

If you need help . . .

Words to find: rate, comprehension, vocabulary, context, synonym, antonym, homonym, phonics, consonant, vowel, blend, syllables, prefix, suffix, attack, compound, appreciation, summarize, inference, discrimination, oral, silent, characterization, meaning, glossary, contraction, word.

READING STUDY SKILLS COMPETENCY REVIEW

1. Put these words in alphabetical order by writing the numbers 1-6 in the proper blanks.

   __ class   __ cub
   __ chair   __ cent
   __ come   __ curl

2. Circle the words that would not be found on the dictionary page containing the guide words *pat* and *pep*.

   pet   pizza
   pick   quell
   peck   pool

3. Draw a line under the word that would not be found in a dictionary of musical terms.

   lyrics
   motorcycle
   rhythm

4. Draw a circle around the one source in which book titles can be found.

   telephone book
   card catalog
   atlas

5. Draw a line from each phonetic symbol to its definition.

   short vowel   ´
   long vowel   ˘
   accented syllable   ‐

6. Draw a line through the information that could not be found in an encyclopedia.

   capital city of Mexico
   a telephone number
   information about elephants

7. Circle the word that tells one thing that can be found in a thesaurus.

   synonyms
   ducks
   baseball players

8. Draw a line under the information that could not be found in a catalog, magazine or newspaper.

   the price of shoes
   today's weather forecast
   your teacher's birthday

9. Draw a line under the information that would not be found in the Table of Contents of a book.

   chapter titles
   page numbers
   copyright date

10. Circle the information that could be found in the glossary of a book.

   author's name
   definition of important words
   number of pages in the book

11. Draw a circle around the information that would not be found in a library card catalog.

> title of book
> author of book
> author's mother's name

12. Draw a line through the information that you would not expect to find on a city map.

> street names
> names of the world's oceans
> rivers and lakes

13. Draw a circle around the information that could be found on a globe.

> the population of India
> the ocean directly north of the Soviet Union
> a picture of the United Nations Building

14. Draw a line through the information you could not find on a graph showing the height of every member of a fifth grade class.

> the shortest boy
> the tallest girl
> the girl with the longest hair

15. Draw lines to connect each punctuation mark with its correct usage definition.

> ? separates words in a series
> , shows excitement
> ! asks a question

16. Draw a line under the information that would not be included in an outline of a book.

> major events
> main characters
> author's dedication

17. Draw a circle around the information that would not be included in a report on the history of Valentine's Day.

> where the holiday originated
> how celebration customs have changed
> the price of candy hearts

18. Draw a line through the process that would not be used in skimming a newspaper article.

> looking for key words and phrases
> looking for headlines
> reading each word in every paragraph

19. Draw a circle around the process that would not be used in making a factual report on Africa.

> estimating the population of Africa
> reading reference books to verify all facts
> supplying diagrams and pictures to support facts

SKILLSTUFF

Answer Key & Glossary

READING

ANSWERS FOR COMPETENCY REVIEWS

I. Word Recognition Skills

1. cry/y; kite/ie; frighten/igh
2. que; lot; kit
3. knife
4. play
5. added
6. bloat; drip; plant
7. come (coming)
8. hop (hopping)
9. tape
10. used
11. cotton
12. vegetable
13. pre-
14. able
15. excitement
16. international
17. kicking
18. Mister/Mr.; Monday/Mon.; Mistress/Mrs.
19. campground
20. . . . he doesn't care . . .
21. through

II. Word Usage Skills

1. shutter; steps; leaves
2. whistled
3. wintry; wind; icy; storm
4. deceased
5. living
6. poured
7. quietly
8. frightened
9. A driving rain poured
10. eerie
11. earth
12. yellow
13. attempted
14. eroding
15. forward
16. forbidding; sullen
17. mellow

III. Comprehension Skills

1. Sentences 1, 2, and 9
2. Sentence 4
3. Sentence 1
4. olive green prison uniforms
5. . . . police helicopters joined the the search . . .
6. Just after noon today, three prisoners escaped from the State Prison.
7. Sentences 1, 7 and 9
8. . . . have served 13 years of their sentences.
9. an airplane
10. . . . gathered their things and ran for shelter.
11. . . . children screamed for help.
12. My mother said we were going to have hamburgers for dinner.
13. All soldiers are strong and brave.
14. still; gaunt; stark
15. surly and selfish, egocentric
16. 3, 1, 2

IV. Reading Study Skills

1. cent; chair; class; come; cub; curl
2. pick; pizza; quell; pool
3. motorcycle
4. card catalog
5. ˘/short vowel; ‾/long vowel; ´/accented syllable
6. a telephone number
7. synonyms
8. your teacher's birthday
9. copyright date
10. definition of important words
11. author's mother's name
12. names of the world's oceans
13. the ocean north of the Soviet Union
14. the girl with the longest hair
15. ?/asks a question: ,/separates words in a series; !/shows excitement
16. author's dedication
17. the price of candy hearts
18. reading each word in every article
19. estimating the population of Africa

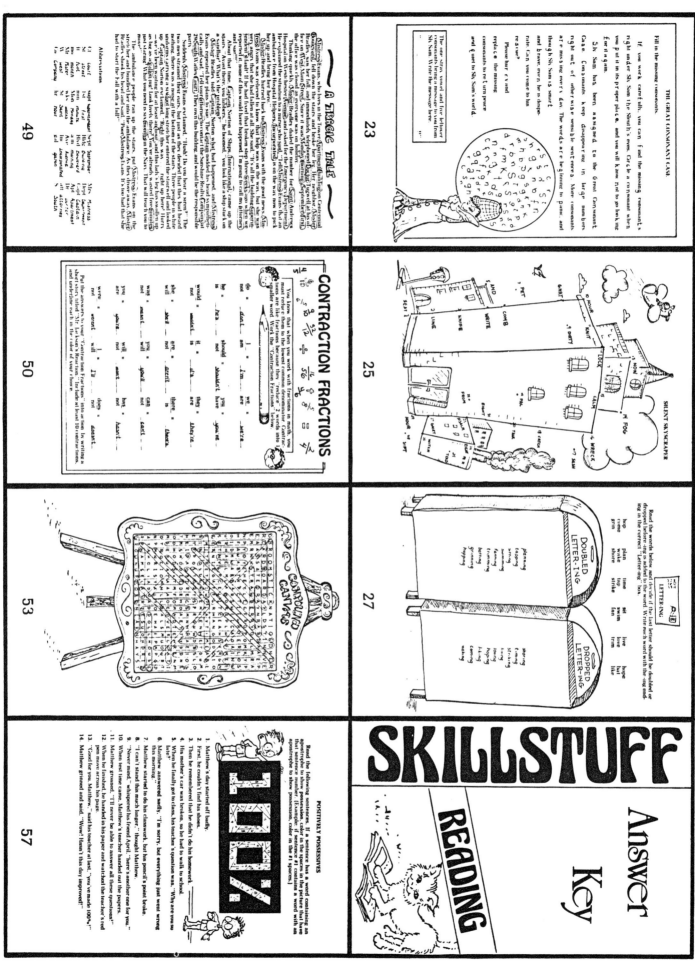

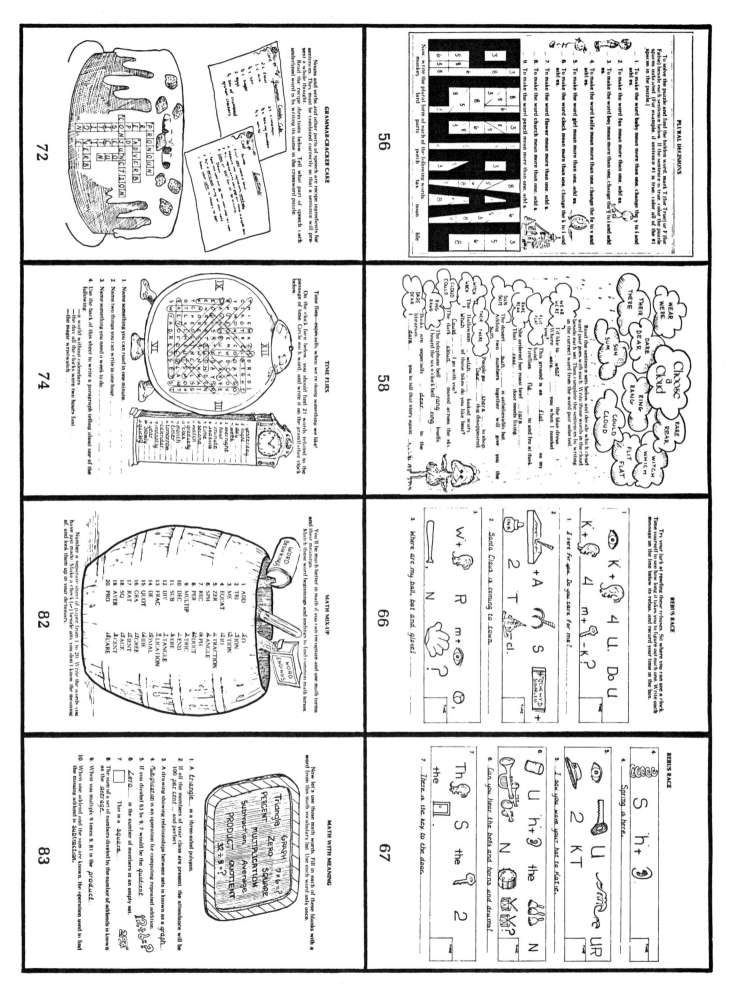

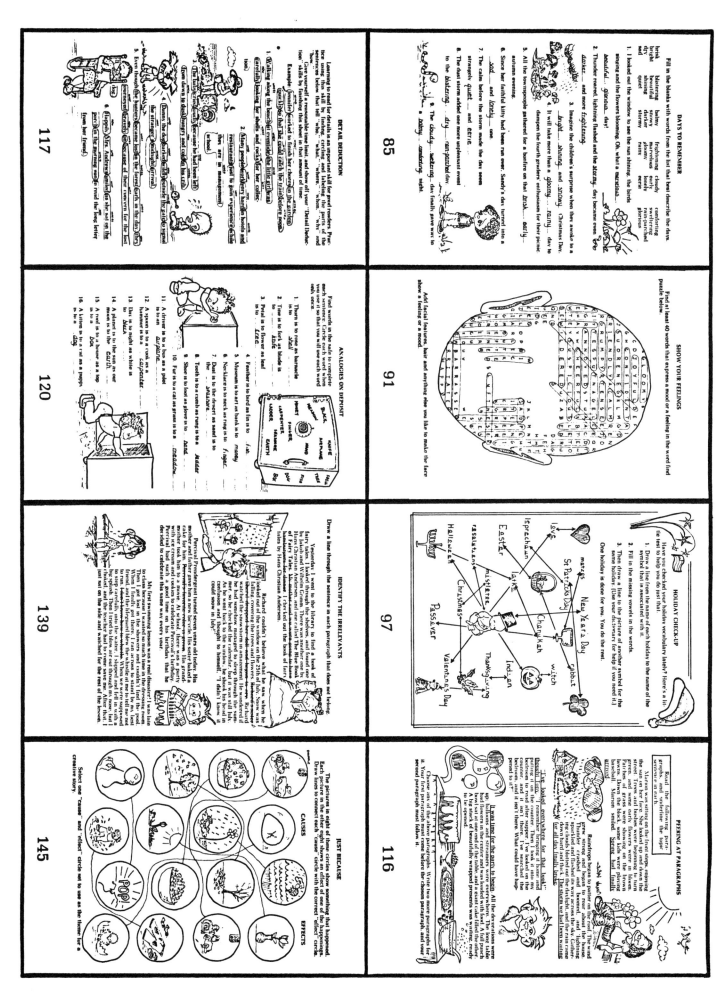

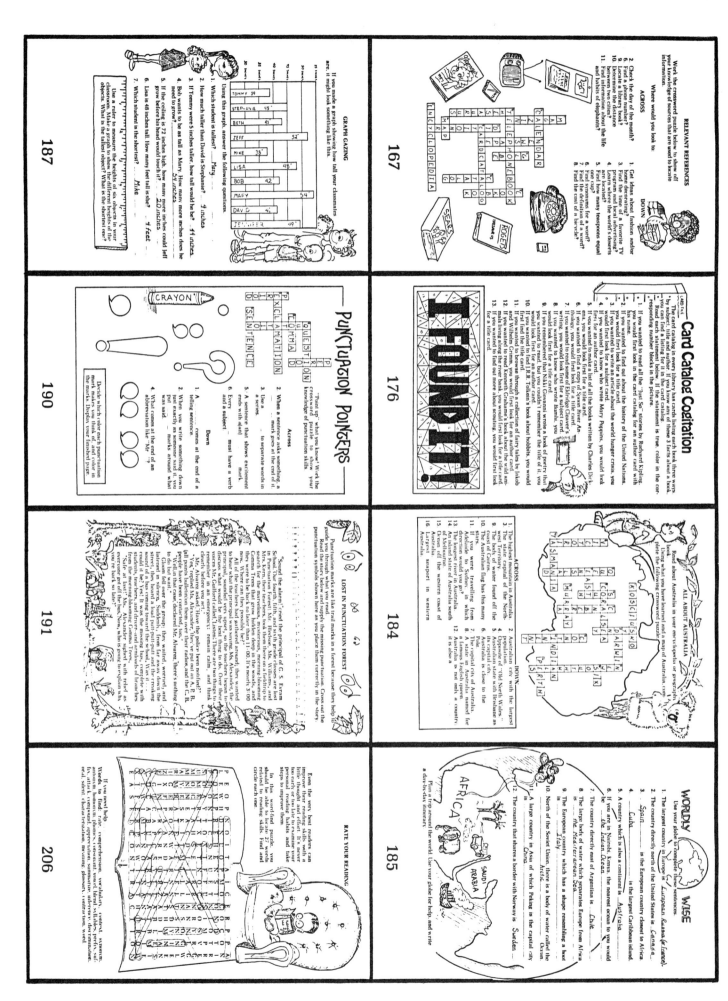

RELEVANT REFERENCES

Work the crossword puzzle below to show off your knowledge of sources that are used to locate information.

Where would you look to:

ACROSS
2. Check the day of the month?
5. Find ideas about fashion and/or home decorating?
9. Find a phone number?
10. Locate a library book?
11. Determine the distance between two cities?

DOWN
1. Get ideas about fashion and/or home decorating?
3. Find the time of a favorite TV program and local advertising?
4. Learn where the world's deserts are located?
6. Find how many teaspoons equal one cup?
7. Find synonyms for a word?
8. Find the definition of a word?
8. Find the cost of a bicycle?

Answers include: CALENDAR, ENCYCLOPEDIA, TELEPHONEBOOK, CARDCATALOG, ROGET, SEARS

167

Card Catalog Cogitation

The card catalog in every library has cards listing each book, three ways. Read each statement below. If the statement is true, color in the corresponding number blocks in the picture.

1. If you wanted to read all the "Just So" stories by Rudyard Kipling, you would first look in the card catalog with his name.
2. If you wanted to find out about the history of the United Nations, you would first look for a title card.
3. If you wanted to read about the world hunger crisis, you would first look for a subject card.
4. If you wanted to know who wrote Mary Poppins, you would look first for an author card.
5. If you wanted to make a list of all the books written by Charles Dickens, you would look first for a title card.
6. If you wanted to read a copy of Swan River Anthology, you would first look for a title card.
7. If you wanted to read some of Eldridge Cleaver's writing, you would look first for a subject card.
8. If you wanted to know who wrote Bambi, you would look first for an author card.
9. If you remember that Nikki Giovanni wrote a book of poetry that you couldn't read, but you remember the title of it, you would look first for an author card.
10. If you wanted to browse through a collection of fairy tales by Jakob and Wilhelm Grimm, you would first look for an author card.
11. If you wanted to read Kenneth Grahame's book, about the wild animals living along the river bank, you would first look for a title card.
12. If you wanted to read J.R.R. Tolkien's book about hobbits, you would first find the title card.
13. If you wanted to find out more about scouting, you would first look for a title card.

I FOUND IT!

176

ALL ABOUT AUSTRALIA

Read about Australia in your encyclopedia and a map of Australia, complete the following crossword puzzle!

ACROSS
2. The highest mountain in Australia.
3. The state capital of the North.
7. The body of water found off the coast of Cairns.
8. The Australian flag has this many stars.
10. Adelaide is travelling from direction to Sydney.
11. The longest river in Australia.
14. An island state of Australia south.
15. Ocean off the western coast of Australia.
16. Largest seaport in western Australia.

DOWN
1. Australian city with the largest population (Old North Wales).
4. Australian state with Brisbane as its capital city.
5. Australia is close to the equator.
6. Australia is a city.
9. A state on Australia named for a famous English queen.
12. Australia is much a country; it is also a

184

WORLDLY WISE

Plan your globe to complete these sentences.

1. The largest country in Europe is _European Russia (& France)._
2. The country directly north of the United States is _Canada._
3. _Spain_ is the European country closest to Africa.
4. _Cuba_ is the largest Caribbean island.
5. If you are in Nairobi, Kenya, the nearest ocean to you would be _the Indian Ocean._
6. The country directly east of Argentina is _Chile._
7. The large body of water which separates Europe from Africa is the _Mediterranean Sea._
8. The European country which has a shape resembling a boot is _Italy._
9. North of the Soviet Union, there is a body of water called the _Arctic_ Ocean.
10. The country that shares a border with Norway is _Sweden._

Even the very best readers can improve their reading skills. It's never too early or too late to examine your personal reading habits and take steps to improve them.

RATE YOUR READING

In this word-find puzzle, you should be able to locate 27 words related to reading skills. Find and circle each one.

If you need help, find:
Words to find: comprehension, vocabulary, context, skimming, appreciation, enjoyment, vowel, syllable, prefix, suffix, attack, compound, appreciation, inference, determination, oral, silent, characterization, meaning, glossary, contraction, word

185

206

GRAPH GAZING

If you made a graph showing how tall your classmates are, it might look something like this.

TOMMY	39"
STEP-ANIE	45"
BETH	43"
JEFF	52"
MIKE	38"
LISA	48"
BOB	42
MARY	54"
DAVID	41
JENNIFER	49"

Using this graph, answer the following questions.

1. Which student is tallest? _Mary._
2. How much taller than David is Stephanie? _4 inches._
3. If Tommy were 5 inches taller, how tall would he be? _44 inches._
4. Bob wants to be as tall as Mary. How many more inches does he need to grow? _54 inches._
5. If the ceiling is 72 inches high, how many more inches could Jeff grow before his head would touch it?
6. Lisa is 48 inches tall. How many feet tall is she? _4 feet._
7. Which student is the shortest? _Mike_

Use a ruler to measure the heights of six objects in your classroom. Make a graph to show the different heights of the objects. What is the tallest object? What is the shortest one?

187

PUNCTUATION POINTERS

"Point up" what you know! Work the crossword puzzle below to show your knowledge of punctuation skills.

Across
2. When a sentence asks something, a mark goes at the end of it.
3. Use a _____ to separate words in a series.
5. A sentence that shows excitement ends with a(an) _____.
6. Every _____ must have a verb and a subject.

Down
1. _____ comes at the end of a telling sentence.
4. When you write something down just exactly as someone said it, you put _____ marks around what was said.
7. What comes at the end of an abbreviation like "Mr."?

Answers: QUESTION, PERIOD, COMMA, EXCLAMATION, SENTENCE, CRAYON

Decide which rider each punctuation mark makes you think of, and color in the marks. Display your finished page.

190

LOST IN PUNCTUATION FOREST

Punctuation marks are like trail marks in a forest because they help to guide you through what you read. Read the story below and supply the missing punctuation. Cross out as you place them correctly in the story.

"Sound the alarm!" cried the principal of G. S. Evram School. Our fourth, fifth, and sixth grade classes are and two years...

191

214

GLOSSARY

Abbreviation—a shortened form of a word which usually ends with a period.
Example: Mister—Mr.

Analogy—a form of logical inference in which two dissimilar or unrelated things are compared.
Example: Green is to grass as blue is to sky.

Antonym—a word that means the opposite of a given word.
Examples: hot—cold
day—night

Auditory Association—the ability to interpret, integrate and use what is heard.

Auditory Closure—the ability to blend sounds to identify the whole word.

Auditory Discrimination—the ability to hear differences and similarities in sounds.

Auditory Perception—the sensory ability to receive, arrange and interpret auditory stimuli.

Compound Word—a word formed by combining two separate words to create a new word.
Examples: snowflake, airplane

Consonant—the letters b, c, d, f, g, h, j, k, l, m, n, p, q, r, s, t, v, w, x, y and z of the English Alphabet.

Consonant Blend—a combined sound of two or three consonants which are written or spoken together. Each of the consonants has a separate sound, but when the letters are pronounced, they are blended together to make one sound.
Examples: black, glad, think

Consonant Blend, Final—a consonant blend which occurs at the end of a word.
Examples: left, bank

Consonant Blend, Initial—a consonant blend which occurs at the beginning of a word.
Example: train

Consonant, Final—a single consonant at the end of a word.
Examples: at, cap

Consonant, Initial—a single consonant at the beginning of a word.
Examples: boy, table

Consonant, Silent—a consonant within a word that does not make a speech sound.
Examples: know (silent k)
night (silent gh)
subtle (silent b)

Consonant Sound, Variant—a consonant which has more than one pronunciation sound.
—Hard and Soft C: The Hard C sounds like K in front of a, o, u and blends. The Soft C sounds like S in front of e, i or y.
Examples: cat—Hard C
city—Soft C
—Hard and Soft G: The Hard G sounds like G in front of a, o, u and the blends gl- and gr-. The Soft G sounds like J in front of e, i, o or y.
Examples: gun—Hard G
gypsy—Soft G

Contraction—a word formed by joining two words together but leaving out one (or more) of the letters and replacing it with an apostrophe.
Example: are not—aren't

Digraph, Consonant—two consonants that appear together in a word which form a single speech sound.
Examples: chirp, what, bang

Digraph, Vowel—two vowels that appear together within a word which form a single speech sound.
Examples: mean, eight, stood

Diphthong—a speech sound that begins with one vowel sound and moves quickly to the adjacent vowel sound within the same syllable.
Examples: boy, caught

English Alphabet—the 26 letters, arranged in the order fixed by custom, that are used to write words in English.

Heteronym—a word that has the same spelling as another word, but is pronounced differently and has a different meaning.
Examples: wind—wind
project—project

Homonym—a word that sounds like another word, but has a different meaning and a different spelling.
Examples: pair—pear
blew—blue

Idiom—a set of words, a phrase or a sentence that has a meaning peculiar to itself which is different from the literal meaning of the individual words.
Example: I'm on top of the world.

Phoneme—the smallest unit of sound in a language.
Examples: sound of **b** as in **but**
sound of **m** as in **mat**

Phonetics—the science of speech sounds.

Phonics—the study of sounds as related to reading and enunciation.

Phonogram—a character or symbol that represents a speech sound.
Examples: o—long o
ə—schwa

Prefix—a set of letters placed before a root word to form a word with a new meaning.
Example: **un**tie

Rhyming Word—a word that is similar in ending sound to another word.
Examples: pail—mail
deep—creep

Root Word—a word from which other words are formed by adding a prefix and/or suffix.
Examples: **re**paint, **rain**ing

Suffix—a letter or syllable placed at the end of a root word to form a word with a new meaning.
Example: high**est**

Syllable—a letter or group of letters pronounced as a part of a word or a whole word.

Syllable, Closed—a syllable ending in a consonant which usually contains a short vowel sound.
Example: **nim**-ble

Syllable, Open—a syllable ending in a vowel which usually has a long vowel sound.
Example: **ta**-ble

Synonym—a word that has a meaning similar to or the same as another word.
Example: sick—ill

Vowel—the letters a, e, i, o and u (and sometimes y and w) in the English Alphabet. Every word or syllable must contain at least one vowel.

Vowel, Long—a vowel which has the speech sound of that letter in the English Alphabet.

Vowel, "R" Controlled—a vowel sound that is changed or controlled by the letter "R" which follows the vowel.
Examples: hard, girl, herd

Vowel, Short—a vowel which has a speech sound of relatively short duration, usually found in words of one syllable that contain only one vowel, or in syllables that end with a consonant.
Examples: back, battle

Vowel, Silent—a vowel that does not make a speech sound of its own, but usually makes the vowel that precedes it long.
Examples: cak**e**, shon**e**

READING

TABLE OF CONTENTS

SHORT A WORDS

add	chance	grab	pad	slap
after	clam	grand	pal	slat
ant	clamp	grant	pan	snag
ask	clasp	grass	pant	snap
at	class	had	pass	span
ax	crack	ham	past	splash
back	cramp	hand	pat	stab
bad	crash	handle	plan	stack
bag	dad	hat	plant	stamp
bat	dam	jab	quack	tab
bath	damp	jam	rack	tacks
black	dance	lab	raft	tag
bland	dash	lamb	rag	tan
brand	drab	lamp	ram	task
brass	fact	land	ran	than
cab	fan	last	rang	that
camp	fat	mad	rap	track
can	flag	man	rat	trap
candle	flat	map	sack	trash
cap	gal	mask	sad	vamp
cash	gap	master	sand	van
cast	gas	match	sang	vast
cat	glance	nag	scab	wax
catch	glass	nap	scrap	yam
champ	gnat	pack	slab	

SHORT E WORDS

beck	dwell	ledge	quench	them
bed	edge	left	red	then
beg	egg	leg	rent	vent
bell	elbow	less	rest	vest
bench	ever	let	scent	vet
bend	fed	level	sell	vex
bent	fell	men	send	web
best	fence	mend	sent	wed
bet	fetch	mess	shed	wedge
bled	fleck	met	shell	well
blend	fled	neck	shred	went
bless	flesh	nest	sled	wept
bred	fresh	net	sledge	west
cell	gem	never	slept	wet
cent	get	next	smell	when
center	hedge	pebble	sped	wreck
chest	helmet	peck	spell	wrench
clef	help	peg	spend	yell
crest	hem	pen	spent	yelp
deck	hen	pep	stress	yes
dell	jelly	pest	swept	yet
dense	jest	pet	tell	zest
dent	jet	pledge	ten	
desk	kept	press	tent	
dress	led	quell	test	

2

SHORT I WORDS

bib	ill	pinch	strip
bid	in	pit	swim
big	inch	rib	thin
bill	jig	rid	thing
bin	kick	rift	this
brick	kid	rig	tickle
bridge	king	rill	till
chick	kiss	rim	tin
chin	knit	rip	tip
dig	lid	risk	twin
dill	lift	ship	twist
dim	limb	shrill	vim
dip	lint	sick	vision
dish	lip	sift	whim
fib	list	silk	whip
fig	lit	simmer	whiskers
fill	milk	sin	whistle
film	miss	sip	wick
fish	mist	sister	wiff
fist	mister	sit	wig
fix	mitt	six	will
grin	nibble	skill	win
grip	nick	slit	wing
hid	nil	spill	wit
hill	nip	split	with
him	pick	stick	wrist
hint	picnic	still	yip
his	pig	sting	zip
hit	pin	stitch	

SHORT O WORDS

block	cost	hock	monster	shod
bog	cot	hog	mop	shop
bomb	crock	hop	moss	shot
bond	crop	hot	moth	slob
boss	cross	job	nod	slop
bottle	dock	jot	not	slosh
box	dodge	knob	on	slot
broth	dog	knock	ox	smock
chop	doll	knot	plod	smog
clock	dollar	lock	plop	snob
clod	dot	lodge	plot	sob
clog	drop	loft	pocket	sock
clop	flop	log	pod	song
closet	fog	lollipop	pond	spot
cloth	fond	lop	pop	stock
cob	forgot	loss	pot	stop
cock	fox	lost	rob	top
cod	frost	lot	rock	toss
cog	gloss	mob	rod	
common	gob	mock	rot	
con	got	mod	rotten	
cop	hobble	mom	shock	

bluff	fuzz	plum
blunt	glum	plunge
blush	glut	plus
brunch	grub	pulp
buck	grudge	pump
bud	gruff	punch
buff	grump	pup
bug	gull	rub
bum	gum	ruffle
bump	gun	rug
bun	gush	rum
bunch	gut	run
bundle	gutter	rung
bunt	hub	rush
bus	huff	rust
but	hug	rut
buzz	hull	skull
clump	hum	skunk
clutch	humble	slug
crumb	hump	slum
crunch	hunch	slump
crust	hung	sprung
cub	hunt	struck
cuff	husk	stun
cull	hut	stunt
cup	jug	sun
cut	jump	sung
drudge	just	sunk
drug	jut	swung
drum	luck	truck
duck	lug	trunk
dug	lull	trust
dull	lump	tub
dumb	lunch	tuck
dump	lung	tug
dusk	muck	tusk
dust	mud	ugly
fluff	mug	umbrella
flung	mull	uncle
flush	munch	under
fluster	mush	unjust
fudge	must	until
fun	null	up
fund	nut	us
fuss	pluck	

LONG A WORDS (SILENT E)

ace	cave	glade	mistake	shape
agape	chase	glaze	name	skate
age	crate	grace	nape	slate
ale	crave	grade	pace	slave
amaze	date	grape	page	snake
ape	daze	grate	pave	space
ate	deface	grave	place	spade
babe	disgrace	graze	plane	stage
bale	drake	hale	plate	stake
bake	drape	hate	quake	stale
base	engage	haze	race	state
bathe	enrage	jade	rage	stave
blame	evade	knave	rake	take
blaze	exhale	lace	rape	tale
behave	face	lake	rate	tame
brace	fade	lame	rave	tape
brake	fake	lane	sage	thane
brave	fame	late	sake	trace
cage	fate	lathe	sale	trade
cake	flake	mace	same	vale
came	flame	made	sane	vane
cane	gale	make	save	wade
cape	game	male	scrape	wage
case	gate	mane	shade	
	gave	mate	shake	
	gaze	maze	shame	

LONG I WORDS (SILENT E)

abide	grime	price	strive
advice	gripe	prime	swipe
advise	hive	prize	thrice
arrive	ice	rice	thrive
aside	ire	rife	tile
beside	kite	rile	time
bide	knife	ripe	tire
bile	lice	rise	tribe
bite	life	rite	tripe
bribe	lime	scribe	twice
bride	line	shine	vice
brine	live	shrine	vile
chide	mice	shire	vine
chime	mile	sire	vise
chive	mime	size	while
cite	mine	slice	whine
crime	mire	slime	white
fife	mite	smile	wide
file	nice	spice	wife
fine	nine	splice	wine
fire	pile	stile	wipe
five	pine	strife	wire
glide	pipe	stripe	wise

LONG O WORDS (SILENT E)

bode	grope	rode
bone	hole	rope
broke	home	rose
choke	hone	rote
chose	hope	rove
chrome	hose	scope
clone	hove	slope
close	joke	smoke
clothe	lobe	smote
clove	lone	sole
coke	lope	stoke
cone	mode	stole
cope	mole	stone
cove	mope	stove
crone	node	strobe
dole	nose	strode
dome	note	stroke
dope	phone	those
dose	poke	throne
dote	pole	tone
doze	pope	tote
drone	pose	vote
drove	probe	woke
froze	prone	yoke
globe	quote	zone
	robe	

LONG U WORDS (SILENT E)

brute	dude	huge	prude	spruce
butte	duke	jute	prune	tube
chute	dune	mule	puke	tune
crude	dupe	mute	pure	yule
cube	flute	nude	rule	
cute	fume		ruse	

FINAL Y

Long E

alley	factory	hockey	lucky	quickly	
army	fairy	honey	memory	rocky	
baby	family	hungry	money	stingy	
bunny	fancy	hurry	mystery	study	
bury	funny	ivory	naughty	surgery	
busy	furry	ivy	navy	taffy	
canary	fury	jockey	nursery	tiny	
city	glory	journey	party	twenty	
country	grocery	jury	penny	ugly	
county	happy	lady	plenty	very	
drowsy	hardy	lazy	pony	weary	
easy	heavy	liberty	poppy	zany	

Long I

buy
by
cry
dry
fly
fry
my
ply
pry
shy
sky
sly
spry
spy
sty
try
why
wry

VOWEL DIGRAPHS (FIRST VOWEL LONG)

-AI- (long a)

aid	drain	lain	quail	tail
aide	fail	maid	quaint	taint
ail	fain	mail	raid	trail
aim	faint	maim	rail	train
bail	faith	main	rain	trait
bait	flail	maize	raise	twain
braid	frail	nail	sail	vain
brain	gain	paid	saint	waif
braise	gaily	pail	slain	wail
chain	gait	pain	snail	wain
chaise	grain	paint	staid	waist
claim	hail	plain	stain	wait
daily	jail	plait	strain	waive
dainty	laid	praise	strait	

-AY- (long a)

bay	dray	hay	pay	spray
bray	flay	jay	play	splay
clay	fray	lay	ray	stay
crayon	gay	may	say	stray
day	gray	nay	slay	tray
				way

-EA- (long e)

beach	crease	heal	peach	seat
bead	deal	heap	peak	sneak
beak	dean	heat	peal	speak
beam	decease	heave	peat	squeak
bean	decrease	knead	plea	squeal
beast	disease	lead	plead	steal
beat	dream	leaf	please	steam
bleach	each	leak	pleat	streak
bleak	eagle	lean	preach	tea
bleat	ease	leap	reach	teach
breach	east	least	read	teak
cease	eat	leave	real	team
cheap	feast	meal	ream	treat
clean	feat	mean	reap	tweak
cleat	freak	meat	scream	veal
cleave	gleam	neat	sea	weak
creak	glean	pea	seal	yeast
cream	grease	peace	seam	zeal

7

VOWEL DIGRAPHS (FIRST VOWEL LONG)

-EE- (long e)

bee	feed	keen	screen	
beech	feel	knee	seed	steel
beep	feet	lee	seep	steep
between	flee	leech	seek	steeple
bleed	fleece	leek	seem	street
breech	fleet	meek	seen	teem
breed	free	meet	sheen	teeth
breeze	freed	need	sheep	thee
cheek	freeze	peek	sheet	three
cheese	geese	peel	sleep	tree
creed	glee	peep	sleet	tweed
creek	greed	peeve	sleeve	weed
creep	green	preen	sneeze	weep
deed	greet	queen	speech	wheel
deep	heed	reed	speed	wheeze
deem	heel	reek	spleen	
eel	jeep	reel	spree	
fee	keel	screech	squeeze	

-OA- (long o)

afloat	croak	load	oaken	shoat
bloat	float	loaf	oat	soak
boast	foal	loafer	oath	soap
boat	foam	loam	poach	throat
broach	gloaming	loan	poacher	toad
cloak	gloat	loath	roach	toast
coach	goad	loathe	road	toaster
coal	goal	loaves	roam	whoa
coast	goat	moan	roan	
coaster	groan	moat	roast	
coat	groat	oaf	roaster	
coax	hoax	oak	shoal	

8

VOWEL DIGRAPHS

-OO- (boot)

bloom	hoot	scoop
boom	loom	shoot
boot	loop	sloop
boost	loose	spoof
booster	loot	spool
brood	mood	spoon
cool	moose	smooth
coop	noon	snooze
doom	noose	stool
drool	pool	stoop
droop	proof	swoop
food	roof	too
fool	room	toot
gloom	roost	tooth
goose	rooster	troop
groom	root	whoop
hoop	school	zoo

-OO- (book)

book	good	poor
boor	hood	rook
brook	hoof	shook
cook	hook	soot
cookies	look	stood
crook	moor	took
foot	nook	wool

-UE

acrue	due	gruel
blue	duel	hue
clue	ensue	rue
cruel	fuel	sue
cue	glue	true

9

DIPHTHONGS

-AU-

applause
auction
audience
audit
audition
aught
augment
august
auk
austere
authentic
author
auto
autograph
autumn
bauble
because
caucus
caught
caulk

cause
caustic
caution
clause
daub
daughter
daunt
exaust
fault
faun
flaunt
fraud
fraught
gaudy
gaunt
gauze
haughty
haul
haunch
haunt

jaunt
laud
launch
launder
laundry
laurel
maul
naughty
nausea
pauper
paunch
pause
sauce
saunter
taught
taunt
taut
vault

-AW-

awe
awesome
awning
bawl
brawl
brawn
caw
claw
craw
crawl
dawn
draw
drawl
drawn
fawn
flaw
gnaw
hawk
hawthorn
jaw
law

lawn
lawyer
mohawk
paw
pawl
pawn
prawn
raw
saw
scrawl
shawl
slaw
spawn
sprawl
squaw
straw
thaw
trawl
withdraw
yawn

-EW-

anew
askew
bedew
blew
brew
chew
clew
crew

dew
drew
flew
grew
hew
jewel
knew
lewd

mew
new
newt
pew
renew
review
shrew
skew

slew
spew
stew
strew
threw
view
yew

-OI-

adjoin
anoint
appoint
asteroid
avoid
boil
broil
choice
coil
coin
conjoint
counterpoint

despoil
devoid
disappoint
disjointed
embroil
enjoin
foil
foist
hoist
join
joint
joist

loin
moil
moist
noise
oil
ointment
purloin
point
poise
quoin
quoit
recoil

rejoice
rejoin
roil
soil
spoil
subjoin
toil
turmoil
voice
void

DIPHTHONGS

-OU-

abound
about
account
aground
aloud
amount
announce
astound
avouch
becloud
blouse
bough
bounce
bound
bout
cloud
clout
compound
confound
couch
count
crouch
denounce
devour
devout
discount
doubt
douse
enshroud
expound
flounce
flounder
flour
flout
foul
found
fount
gout
grouch
ground
grouse
grout
hound
house
impound
joust
loud
louse
lout
mound
mouse
mouth
noun
ouch
ounce
our
out
paramount
pouch
pound
pout
profound
pronounce
rebound
remount
renounce
resound
round
route
scour
scout
shout
shroud
slouch
sound
sour
south
spout
sprout
stout
surmount
surround
thou
tout
trounce
trout
vouch
without
wound

-OW-

allow
bow
bower
brow
brown
chow
chowder
clown
cow
cower
cowl
crowd
crown
down
drown
endow
flower
fowl
frown
glower
gown
growl
how
howitzer
howl
jowl
now
owl
plow
pow
powder
power
prow
prowl
renown
row
scow
shower
sow
town
vow
wow
yowl

-OY-

annoy
boy
cloy
convoy
coy
decoy
deploy
destroy
employ
enjoy
gargoyle
joy
loyal
ploy
royal
toy
troy

11

R CONTROLLED WORDS

-AR-

afar	carnation	far	march	shark
arc	carp	farm	mark	sharp
are	carpet	gar	market	smart
ark	cart	garb	mart	spar
arm	carton	garment	par	spark
art	cartoon	guard	parcel	star
bar	carve	hard	parch	starch
barb	char	hark	pardon	stark
bard	charcoal	harm	park	start
bargain	charge	harmony	part	tar
barge	charm	harp	partridge	tart
bark	chart	jar	party	tsar
barn	dark	lard	radar	yard
car	darn	large	sardine	yarn
card	dart	lark	scar	
cardinal	depart	mar	scarf	

-ER-

after	jerk	perfect	pert	stern
berth	jersey	perform	pertinent	summer
clerk	merchant	perfume	reverse	supper
cover	mercury	perhaps	rubber	swerve
enter	mercy	perjury	runner	teacher
farmer	mermaid	perk	serf	term
fern	miserable	permanent	serge	terminal
germ	nerve	permission	sermon	termite
hammer	offer	permit	serpent	tern
her	percale	perplex	servant	terrain
herb	percent	persist	serve	verse
herd	perception	person	service	winter
hermit	perch	perspire	silver	wonder
hunter	percussion	persuade	sitter	

-IR-

affirm	dirt	girt	skirt	thirty
birch	fir	girth	smirch	thirst
bird	firm	irk	smirk	twirl
birth	first	mirth	squirrel	whir
chirp	firth	quirk	squirt	whirl
circle	flirt	shirk	stir	
circus	gird	shirt	swirl	
dirk	girl	sir	third	

R CONTROLLED WORDS

-OR-

abhor	for	normal	sport
abort	ford	north	store
absorb	forge	or	stork
accord	fork	orb	storm
adorn	form	porch	sword
assort	forth	pork	thorn
bore	glory	port	torch
born	gorge	record	tore
chord	horn	report	torn
chore	horse	score	tornado
consort	ignore	scorn	tort
cord	important	shore	worn
core	lord	short	
cork	lorn	snore	
corn	morn	sore	
distort	nor	sort	

-UR-

blur	cursive	purge	surround
blurt	curt	purl	surtax
burden	curtain	purple	survey
burdock	curtsy	purpose	survive
burg	curve	purr	turban
burglar	fur	purse	turbine
burlap	furl	return	turbulent
burn	furnish	slur	turf
burnt	furniture	spur	turkey
burr	furrow	spurn	turmoil
burro	further	spurt	turn
burrow	hurdle	surf	turnip
burst	hurl	surface	turpentine
church	hurricane	surge	turquoise
churn	hurry	surgeon	turret
cur	hurt	surmise	turtle
curb	hurtle	surname	urban
curd	lurch	surpass	urchin
curfew	lurk	surplus	urge
curl	nurse	surprise	urgent
current	nursery	surrender	urn
curse	nurture	surrey	

CONSONANT BLENDS

BL-

blab	blaze	blimp	blob	blotter
black	blazer	blind	block	blouse
bladder	bleach	blinder	blockade	blow
blade	bleacher	blindfold	bloke	blower
blame	bleak	blink	blond	blubber
blanch	bleary	blintz	blood	blue
bland	bleat	blip	bloodhound	blueprint
blank	bleed	bliss	bloodshed	bluff
blanket	blemish	blister	bloody	blunder
blare	blend	blithe	bloom	blunt
blarney	blender	blithering	blooper	blur
blast	bless	blitz	blossom	blurb
blat	blew	blizzard	blot	blurt
blatant	blight	bloat	blotch	blush

BR-

brace	brat	breeze	brink	brood
bracelet	brave	brevity	brisk	brook
bracken	brawl	brew	bristle	broom
bracket	brawn	briar	britches	broth
brad	bray	bribe	brittle	brother
brag	brazen	brick	broach	brought
braid	brazier	bride	broad	brow
braille	breach	bridge	brocade	brown
brain	breadth	bridle	broccoli	brownie
braise	break	brief	brochure	browse
brake	breakfast	brier	brogue	bruin
bramble	breast	brig	broil	bruise
bran	breath	brigade	broiler	brunch
branch	breathe	brigand	broke	brunt
brand	bred	bright	broken	brush
brandish	breech	brilliant	broker	brusque
brandy	breeches	brim	bronco	brutal
brash	breed	brine	bronze	brute

CL-

clack	clarinet	clef	clinic	clot
clad	clarity	cleft	clink	cloth
claim	clash	clemency	clip	clothe
clam	clasp	clench	clipper	clothes
clamber	class	clergy	clique	cloud
clammy	classic	clerical	cloak	clout
clamor	classify	clerk	clobber	clove
clamp	clatter	clever	clock	clover
clan	clause	click	clod	clown
clang	claw	client	clog	club
clank	clay	cliff	cloister	cluck
clap	clean	climate	clone	clue
clapboard	cleanser	climax	clop	clump
clapper	clear	climb	close	clumsy
claptrap	cleat	clinch	closet	cluster
clarify	cleave	cling	closure	clutch

CR-

crab	cravat	creepy	crisp	crow
crack	crave	cremate	critic	crowd
cracker	craw	crepe	critical	crown
crackle	crawl	crept	criticize	crucial
cradle	crayfish	crescent	critter	crucify
craft	crayon	cress	croak	crud
crafty	craze	crest	crochet	crude
crag	crazy	crevasse	crock	cruel
cram	creak	crevice	crocodile	cruet
cramp	cream	crew	crocus	cruise
cranberry	crease	crib	crone	crumb
crane	create	crick	crony	crumble
cranial	creation	cricket	crook	crumpet
crank	creator	crier	crooked	crumple
cranky	creature	crime	croon	crunch
cranny	credit	crimp	crop	crusade
crappie	creed	crimson	croquet	crutch
crash	creek	cringe	cross	crux
crass	creel	crinkle	crouch	cry
crate	creep	cripple	croup	crypt

DR-

drab	drape	dregs	drivel	drowsy
dracma	drastic	drench	driver	drub
draft	drat	dress	drizzle	drudge
draftsman	draw	dresser	droll	drug
drafty	drawer	dressing	dromedary	druid
drag	drawl	drew	drone	drum
dragon	drawn	dribble	drool	drunk
drain	dray	drier	droop	dry
drake	dread	drift	dropper	dryad
dram	dream	drill	drought	dryly
drama	dreamer	drink	drove	
dramatic	dreary	drip	drown	
drank	dredge	drive	drowse	

FL-

flabbergast	flask	flew	floe	flown
flabby	flat	flex	flog	fluctuate
flag	flatten	flexible	flood	flue
flagon	flatter	flick	floor	fluent
flagrant	flaunt	flier	floozy	fluff
flail	flavor	flight	flop	fluid
flair	flaw	flimsy	floral	fluke
flake	flax	flinch	florist	flume
flame	flay	fling	floss	flunk
flamingo	flea	flint	flounce	fluorescent
flammable	fleck	flip	flounder	fluoride
flank	fledgling	flippant	flour	flurry
flannel	flee	flirt	flourish	flush
flap	fleece	flit	flout	flute
flare	fleet	float	flow	flutter
flash	flesh	flock	flower	flux

FR-

fracas	frantic	freight	frill	front
fraction	fraternal	frenzy	fringe	frontier
fracture	fraud	frequent	frisk	frost
fragile	fraught	fresh	fritter	frosty
fragment	fray	fret	frivolous	froth
fragrance	frazzle	friar	frizz	frown
fragrant	freak	friction	frizzle	frozen
frail	freckle	fried	frock	frugal
frame	free	friend	frog	fruit
franc	freedom	frigate	frolic	frustrate
franchise	freeze	fright	from	fry
frank	freezer	frigid	frond	

GL-

glacial	gland	glib	gloat	glossary
glacier	glare	glide	glob	glove
glad	glass	glider	globe	glow
glade	glaze	glimmer	gloom	glucose
gladiator	gleam	glimpse	glorious	glue
gladly	glean	glint	glory	glum
glamour	glee	glisten	gloss	glut
glance	glen	glitter		glutton
				glycerin

GR-

grab	graph	grid	grin	gross
grace	graphic	griddle	grind	grouch
gracious	grapple	grief	grinder	ground
grade	grasp	grievance	grip	group
gradual	grass	grieve	gripe	grouse
graduate	grate	griffin	grisly	grove
graduation	grateful	grill	gristle	grovel
graft	gratify	grim	grit	grow
grain	gratis	grime	gritty	growl
gram	gratitude	grimy	grizzly	grown
grammar	grave	great	groan	growth
granary	gravel	greatly	grocer	grudge
grand	gravity	greed	grog	gruel
granite	gravy	green	groggy	gruff
grant	gray	greet	groin	grumble
granular	graze	grenade	groom	grumpy
grape	grease	grew	groove	grunt
grapefruit	greasy	grey	grope	

CONSONANT BLENDS

PL-

placard	plant	plea	ploy
placate	planter	plead	pluck
place	plaque	pleasant	plug
placement	plasma	please	plum
placid	plaster	pleasure	plumage
plaque	plastic	pleat	plumb
plaid	plate	pledge	plumber
plain	plateau	plentiful	plume
plaint	platform	plenty	plummet
plaintiff	platinum	pliable	plump
plait	platoon	pliant	plunder
plan	platter	pliers	plunge
plane	platypus	plight	plunger
planet	plausible	plod	plunk
plank	play	plop	plural
plankton	player	plot	plus
planner	plaza	plow	plush
			ply

PR-

practical	prestige	privilege	promise
practice	pretend	prize	promote
prairie	pretty	probable	prompt
praise	preview	probably	prone
prance	prey	probe	prong
prank	price	problem	pronounce
prattle	prick	proceed	proof
prawn	prickle	process	prop
pray	pride	procession	propel
prayer	priest	proclaim	proper
preach	prim	produce	property
precinct	prime	profess	propose
precious	primitive	profession	prose
precise	primp	professor	protect
predict	prince	profile	protest
prefer	princess	profit	proud
premise	principal	profound	prove
prepare	print	profuse	prow
present	prior	program	prowl
preserve	prism	progress	prude
president	prison	prohibit	prudent
press	private	project	prune
pressure		prom	pry

CONSONANT BLENDS

SCH-

schedule
scheme
scholar
scholarship
scholastic
school
schooner

SCR-

scrag
scrap
scrape
scratch
scrawl
scrawny
scream
screech
screen
screw
scribble
scribe
scrim
scrimmage
scrimp
script
scrub
scruple
scrutiny

SHR-

shrank
shrapnel
shred
shrew
shrewd
shriek
shrift
shrike
shrill
shrimp
shrine
shrink
shrive
shrivel
shroud
shrub
shrug
shrunk

SK-

skate
skeleton
skeptic
sketch
skew
skewer
ski
skid
skiff
skill
skim
skimp
skin
skip
skirmish
skirt
skit
skulk
skull
skunk
sky

SL-

slab
slack
slacks
slag
slain
slake
slalom
slam
slander
slang
slant
slap
slapstick
slash
slat
slate
slaughter
slave
slavery

slaw
slay
sleazy
sled
sledge
sleek
sleep
sleepy
sleet
sleeve
sleigh
sleight
slender
slept
sleuth
slew
slice
slicer
slick

slicker
slid
slide
slight
slim
slime
sling
slink
slip
slipper
slit
slither
sliver
slob
slobber
slogan
sloop
slop
slope

sloppy
slosh
slot
sloth
slouch
slovenly
slow
sludge
slug
slugger
sluice
slum
slumber
slump
slung
slunk
slur
slurp
slush
sly

SM-

smack	smile	smitten	smote
smart	smirch	smock	smother
smash	smirk	smog	smudge
smear	smit	smoke	smug
smell	smite	smolder	smuggle
smelt	smith	smooth	smut

SN-

snack	sneak	snipe	snout
snail	sneer	snivel	snow
snake	sneeze	snob	snub
snap	snicker	snoop	snuff
snare	sniff	snooze	snuffle
snarl	sniffle	snore	snug
snatch	snip	snort	snuggle

SP-

spa	special	spindle	spud
space	species	spine	spume
spade	specific	spinet	spunk
span	speck	spire	spur
spangle	speckle	spirit	spurt
spank	sped	spit	sputter
spar	speech	spite	spy
spare	speed	spittle	
spark	spell	spoil	
sparkle	spend	spoke	
sparrow	spent	sponge	
sparse	spew	spool	
spasm	splice	spoon	
spat	spider	spoor	
spatter	spike	sport	
spawn	spill	spot	
speak	split	spouse	
spear	spin	spout	

SPL-

splash	spleen	splice	splotch
splatter	splendid	splint	splurge
splay	splendor	split	splutter

SPR-

sprain	spray	spring	sprout
sprang	spread	sprinkle	spruce
sprat	spree	sprint	sprung
sprawl	sprig	sprit	spry

SQU-

squab	squander	squeak	squib
squabble	square	squeal	squid
squad	squash	squeamish	squint
squalid	squat	squeeze	squire
squall	squaw	squelch	squirm
squalor			squirt

ST-

stab	start	step	stork
stable	starve	sterile	storm
stack	stash	stern	story
stadium	state	stew	stout
staff	static	stick	stove
stag	status	stiff	stow
stage	staunch	stifle	stub
stagger	stave	still	stubble
stagnant	stay	stilt	stud
staid	stead	sting	student
stain	steady	stink	stuff
stair	steal	stint	stumble
stake	stealth	stir	stump
stale	steam	stitch	stun
stalk	steed	stock	stung
stall	steel	stair	stunt
stamp	steep	stole	stupid
stand	steeple	stone	sturdy
staple	steer	stood	sty
star	stein	stop	style
starch	stem	store	
stark			

STR-

straddle	straw	strew	stroke
strafe	stray	strict	stroll
straight	streak	stride	strong
strain	stream	strife	strove
strait	street	strike	struggle
strand	strength	string	strut
strangle	stress	strip	
strap	stretch	strike	

CONSONANT BLENDS

SW-

swab	swat	swept	swirl
swag	swath	swift	swish
swain	sway	swig	switch
swallow	swear	swill	swivel
swam	sweat	swim	swoop
swamp	sweep	swindle	sworn
swan	sweet	swine	
swap	swell	swing	
swarm	swelter	swipe	

TR-

trace	trapper	tribute	trooper
track	trash	trick	trophy
tract	trashy	trickle	tropic
traction	travel	tricky	tropical
tractor	traverse	tried	trot
trade	trawl	trifle	trouble
tradition	trawler	trigger	trough
traffic	tray	trillion	trounce
tragedy	tread	trim	trout
tragic	treason	trio	truce
trail	treat	trip	truck
trailer	treaty	tripe	trudge
train	tree	triple	true
trainer	trek	tripod	truly
trait	tremble	trite	trump
traitor	tremor	triumph	trumpet
tramp	trench	trivet	trundle
trample	trend	trivia	trunk
trance	trespass	trivial	truss
transfer	tress	trod	trust
transit	trestle	troll	trusty
transmit	trial	trolley	truth
trap	triangle	trombone	try
trapeze	tribe	troop	tryst

TW-

twang	twentieth	twin	twist
tweak	twenty	twine	twit
tweed	twice	twinge	twitch
tweezers	twiddle	twinkle	twitter
twelfth	twig	twinkling	
twelve	twilight	twirl	

-DGE

abridge
adjudge
alledge
badge
bridge
budge
cadge
dodge
dredge
drudge
edge
fledge
fudge
grudge
hedge
judge
kedge
ledge
lodge
misjudge
nudge
pledge
ridge
sedge
sledge
sludge
smudge
trudge
wedge

-FT

adrift
aft
aloft
cleft
craft
daft
deft
draft
drift
gift
graft
haft
left
lift
loft
oft
raft
rift
shift
soft
swift
theft
thrift
tuft
waft
weft

-LK

bilk
bulk
elk
hulk
milk
silk
sulk
walk

-NT

absent
annoint
appoint
ant
aunt
bent
blunt
brunt
bunt
cent
chant
dent
dint
event
extent
faint
flaunt
flint
footprint
fount
front
gent
glint
grant
grunt
haunt
hint
hunt
indent
invent
jaunt
joint
lent
lint
mint
mount
paint
pant
pent
pint
plant
point
print
punt
quaint
rant
rent
resent
runt
saint
scant
scent
sent
shunt
slant
spent
sprint
squint
stint
stunt
taunt
tent
tint
vent
want
went

-ND

abscond
and
around
band
bend
behind
beyond
bind
bland
blend
blind
blond
bond
bound
brand
command
end
fend
find
fond
found
friend
frond
fund
gland
grand
grind
ground
hand
hind
hound
kind
land
lend
mend
mind
mound
pond
pound
rand
refund
remind
rend
rind
rotund
round
send
sound
spend
stand
strand
tend
trend
vend
wand
wind
withstand
wound

-NG

bang	dong	king	rung	stung
bing	dung	long	sang	sung
bong	fang	lung	sing	swing
bring	fling	pang	slang	ting
clang	gang	ping	sling	wing
cling	gong	pong	sprang	wrong
clung	hang	prong	spring	zing
ding	hung	rang	sting	

-NK

bank	dank	honk	prank	stank
blank	drank	junk	rank	stink
blink	drink	kink	rink	stunk
bonk	drunk	lank	sank	sunk
brink	dunk	link	shank	swank
bunk	fink	mink	sink	tank
clank	flank	pink	slink	wink
clink	flunk	plank	slunk	zonk
clunk	frank	plink	spank	
crank	hank	plunk	spunk	

-PT

abrupt	apt	erupt	opt	swept
accept	corrupt	except	prompt	wept
adapt	crept	inept	rapt	wrapt
adept	crept	interrupt	sept	
adopt	disrupt	kept	slept	

-SP

asp
clasp
crisp
gasp
grasp
hasp
lisp
rasp
wasp
wisp

-ST

aghast	dust	last	roast
beast	east	least	rust
best	exist	lest	test
blast	fast	list	thirst
blest	feast	lost	toast
boast	fest	mast	trust
breast	fist	mist	tryst
bust	frost	most	vast
cast	ghost	must	vest
chest	gist	nest	west
coast	grist	past	wrest
cost	guest	pest	wrist
crest	gust	post	yeast
crust	heist	priest	zest
cyst	host	quest	
disgust	jest	rest	

CH-

chafe	chapter	cheese	chip
chain	charcoal	cherry	chipmunk
chair	charge	chess	chirp
chaise	chariot	chest	chive
chalk	charm	chew	chocolate
challenge	charming	chick	choice
chamber	chase	chicken	choke
champ	chat	chief	chop
champion	chatter	child	chubby
chance	cheap	chill	chuck
change	cheat	chilly	chum
channel	check	chime	chunk
chant	checker	chimney	church
chap	cheek	chin	churn
chapel	cheer	china	

KN-

knack
knapsack
knave
knead
knee
kneel
knell
knelt
knew
knickknack
knife
knight
knit
knob
knock
knoll
knot
know
knowledge
known
knuckle

PH-

phalanx	phoebe
phantasm	phoenix
phantom	phone
pharmacist	phonics
pharmacy	phonograph
pharynx	phony
phase	phosphate
pheasant	photo
phenomenal	photograph
philanthropy	phrase
philosopher	physic
philosophy	physical
phlegm	physician
phlegmatic	physics
phlox	physiology
phobia	physique

TH- (then)

than
that
the
thee
their
them
themselves
then
thence
there
these
they
thine
this
those
thou
though
thus
thy

TH- (thin)

thane	thigh	thorny	thrive
thank	thimble	thorough	throat
thankful	thin	thought	throb
thatch	thing	thousand	throne
theater	think	thrash	throttle
theft	third	thread	through
theme	thirst	threat	throw
thermal	thirsty	three	thrust
thermometer	thirty	threw	thud
thesis	thistle	thrice	thug
thick	thong	thrift	thumb
thief	thorn	thrill	thump
			thunder

CONSONANT DIGRAPHS/INITIAL

WR-

wrack	wriggle
wraith	wright
wrangle	wring
wrap	wrinkle
wrath	wrist
wreak	writ
wreath	write
wreck	writhe
wren	wrong
wrench	wrote
wrest	wrought
wrestle	wrung
wretch	wry

QU-

quack	quest
quaff	question
quail	quibble
quaint	quick
quake	quiet
qualm	quill
quarry	quilt
quart	quince
quartz	quip
quaver	quirk
quay	quite
queasy	quiver
queen	quiz
queer	quoit
quell	quota
quench	quote
query	

WH-

whack	when	whimsical	whist
whale	whence	whine	whistle
wharf	where	whinny	white
what	whether	whip	whither
wheat	whey	whir	whittle
wheedle	which	whirl	whoa
wheel	whiff	whisk	whopper
wheeze	while	whisker	whorl
whelp	whim	whisper	why

CONSONANT DIGRAPHS/MEDIAL OR FINAL

PH-

alphabet	elephant	nymph	trophy
autograph	gopher	orphan	typhoid
dolphin	nephew	triumph	typhoon

CONSONANT DIGRAPH/FINAL

-CH

arch	brunch	ditch	latch	preach	switch
attach	bunch	drench	leech	punch	teach
batch	catch	each	lunch	reach	thatch
beach	church	epoch	march	pitch	touch
beech	cinch	fetch	match	poach	twitch
bench	clench	finch	much	search	vetch
beseech	clinch	fletch	munch	scratch	watch
birch	clutch	flinch	notch	screech	wench
bitch	coach	hatch	perch	sketch	which
bleach	couch	hitch	pinch	snatch	witch
blotch	crotch	hutch	pitch	speech	wrench
botch	crunch	graph	poach	splotch	wretch
breach	crutch	impeach	parch	starch	
breech	detach	inch	patch	stich	
broach	dispatch	itch	peach	stretch	

-CK

					-GH	-LK
back	fleck	pack	snack	cough	balk
black	flick	peck	sock	enough	bilk
block	flock	pick	speck	laugh	bulk
brick	frock	pluck	stack	rough	calk
buck	hack	pock	stick	tough	caulk
check	hick	prick	stock	trough	chalk
chick	hock	puck	struck		elk
chuck	jack	quack	stuck		folk
clack	kick	quick	suck		hulk
click	knack	rack	tack		milk
clock	knock	rock	thick		silk
cluck	lack	sack	tick		stalk
cock	lick	shack	track		sulk
crack	lock	shock	treck		walk
crick	luck	shuck	trick		whelk
crock	mock	sick	truck		
deck	muck	slack	tuck		
dock	neck	smack	whack		
duck	nick	smock	wick		

-SH

abash	flesh	rash			
afresh	flush	rush			
ash	fresh	sash			
bash	gash	shush			
blush	gnash	slash			
brash	gush	slosh			
brush	hash	slush			
bush	hush	smash			
cash	lash	splash			
clash	lush	squash			
crash	mash	squish			
crush	mesh	stash			
dash	mush	swish			
dish	posh	thrash			
enmesh	plush	thresh			
fish	push	thrush			

-TH

aftermath	hath	quoth	
bath	health	sheath	
beneath	heath	sixth	
birth	herewith	sloth	
both	lath	smith	
breath	length	south	
broth	loth	strength	
cloth	math	teeth	
death	month	troth	
depth	moth	wealth	
fifth	mouth	width	
filth	mirth	with	
forth	ninth	wrath	
froth	oath	wreath	
girth	path		
growth	pith		

26

HARD C

cab	canary	carol	coat	come	country
cabbage	cancel	carpet	cob	comment	coupon
cabin	candle	carrot	cobweb	common	court
cable	candy	carry	cock	company	cover
caboose	cane	cart	cocoa	compass	cow
cactus	cannon	carton	cod	concern	cozy
cage	canoe	carve	code	cone	cub
cake	canteen	case	coffee	conflict	cube
calculate	canyon	cat	coil	contain	cuff
calendar	cape	catalog	coin	contest	culture
calf	capital	catch	cold	control	curse
calm	capsule	caterpillar	collar	cook	custom
calorie	capture	caution	collect	copy	cut
came	car	cave	colony	cork	cute
camel	carbon	caw	color	corn	
camp	card	coach	colt	correct	
campus	care	coal	column	cost	
can	carnival	coast	comb	cottage	

SOFT C

cedar	cinch
ceiling	cinder
celery	cinnamon
cell	circle
cellar	cite
cement	citizen
cent	citrus
center	city
central	civil
cereal	civilization
ceremony	cycle
certain	cyclone
cider	cylinder
cigar	cymbal
cigarette	cypress
	cyst

HARD G

gab	garage	go	gray
gable	garden	goal	green
gadget	gargle	goat	grin
gage	garland	gobble	groan
gain	garlic	goggles	ground
gait	garment	gold	guarantee
galaxy	gas	golf	guard
gale	gash	gone	guess
gall	gasoline	good	guest
gallant	gate	goose	guide
gallery	gather	gopher	guilt
gallon	gauge	gorilla	guitar
gallop	gauze	gossip	gulf
galore	gave	got	gull
galoshes	gay	government	gum
gamble	gaze	gown	gun
game	glad	grade	guppy
gang	globe	grape	gutter
gape	glove	grass	guy

SOFT G

gelatin	gesture
gem	giant
general	ginger
generation	giraffe
generous	gym
gentle	gymnasium
genuine	gyp
geography	gypsy
geometry	gyrate
germ	gyroscope

-GHT LETTER GROUP

blight	flight	might	slight
bought	fought	night	sought
bright	fright	nought	thought
brought	fraught	ought	tight
caught	height	plight	weight
eight	knight	right	wright
fight	light	sight	wrought

These are word pairs that can be used for vocabulary development. The pairs (usually an adjective and a noun) rhyme, and present humorous word pictures. These pairs are sometimes called "Hink Pinks."

To introduce this activity to students, the teacher might ask, "What is a Hink Pink for _____ _____?" (giving the definition words), and then wait for students to supply the rhyming pair.

Example: What is a Hink Pink for an overweight feline?
Hink Pink Answer: A **fat cat**.

The teacher might also ask students to provide the definition of a Hink Pink given.

Example: What is the definition of a **sad dad**?
Answer: An unhappy father.

A "Hink Pink" is used to denote pairs of one syllable each.
A "Hinky Pinky" is used to denote pairs of two syllables each.
A "Hinkety Pinkety" is used to denote pairs of three syllables each.

Pair	Definition
drab-cab	a dreary or dull colored taxi
race-pace	a rate of speed in a running event
black-crack	a dark crevice
glad-lad	a happy boy
bear-scare	a fright caused by a grizzly
rag-bag	a sack for cloth scraps
frail-male	a weak man
pale-whale	a pallid sea mammal
brain-strain	cerebral overwork
fake-snake	a fradulent reptile
chalk-talk	a blackboard discussion
sham-ram	a fake male sheep
damp-camp	a wet tentground
chance-glance	a lucky glimpse
clap-trap	a trick to win applause
grim-hymn	a stern church song
limp-blimp	a dirigible with no air
thin-fin	a fish's narrow "wing"
fine-pine	excellent grade spruce tree
pink-drink	a light red beverage
bright-light	brilliant illumination
brighter-writer	a smarter author
wise-prize	an intelligent award
dock-lock	a key-operated fastening to secure a pier
cold-gold	a cool yellow precious metal
stone-bone	a petrified femur
long-song	a lengthy tune
rude-dude	a crude guy
book-crook	a manuscript thief
broom-room	a closet for storing a sweeping tool
prune-spoon	a utensil used to eat dried plums
loose-noose	a hangman's knot that is not tight

Pair	Definition
harsh-marsh	a rough and unpleasant swamp
smart-start	an intelligent beginning
last-blast	the final explosion
great-date	a wonderful appointment
bath-path	a trail to the shower
fraud-abroad	trickery overseas
brave-slave	a courageous servant
fall-brawl	an autumn fight
wax-tax	a levy on polish
clay-tray	a carrying device made of an earthen material
beach-speech	a talk at the seashore
weak-Greek	a feeble man from Greece
steel-wheel	an iron steering device
dream-scream	a nightmare cry or yell
beast-feast	a monster's banquet
sweet-treat	a sugary feast
deck-check	a ship's flooring inspection
red-shed	a crimson shack
free-bee	a honey-making insect that doesn't cost anything
cheap-sheep	an inexpensive lamb
hen-pen	a cage for chickens
bent-cent	a crooked penny
tent-rent	money paid for canvas lodging
terse-verse	a concise rhyme
wet-pet	a damp domestic animal
blue-hue	an aqua shade
tribe-scribe	the note taker for an Indian group
nice-price	a fair cost
crop-flop	failure of a farm's produce
rope-soap	detergent for cleaning heavy line
floor-store	a shop where flooring is purchased
pork-fork	a utensil to eat pig meat
cross-boss	an angry employer
host-boast	a party giver's bragging
loud-crowd	a noisy group
sound-hound	a healthy dog
flower-shower	a rain of posies
mouse-house	a dwelling for mice
stout-scout	a fat person who is sent out to look ahead
low-blow	a punch under the beltline
slow-crow	a black bird that does not fly fast
brown-crown	a tan headpiece for a ruling person
duck-truck	a vehicle for transporting waterfowl
mud-flood	an inundation of water and dirt
fudge-judge	a person who must choose the best chocolate candy
glum-chum	a sad or unhappy friend
fun-run	an enjoyable jog
tall-wall	a high stone fence
skunk-bunk	a bed for a smelly mammal
time-chime	an hour bell
pig-wig	a hog's hair piece
funny-bunny	a humorous rabbit
pure-cure	untainted medicine
mute-lute	a soundless pear-shaped stringed instrument
cute-newt	an attractive land salamander
quick-pick	a rapid selection
dry-fly	a bothersome insect that is not wet

V-CV/OPEN SYLLABLE WORDS

agent	decide	futile	minus	silence
baby	defeat	genius	miser	siphon
bacon	defend	glacier	moment	sober
baker	dilate	gopher	motel	soda
basis	diner	gyrate	nature	solo
before	eject	haven	navy	spiral
below	elect	hero	omit	spoken
blatant	erase	hobo	open	tiger
bonus	evade	hotel	oval	vacant
cedar	even	ibex	pilot	vapor
chosen	evil	ibis	polo	veto
cider	fatal	icy	quaver	vocal
climate	favor	label	radar	wager
clover	fever	labor	razor	yodel
cocoa	fiber	lady	recent	zebra
cohort	final	local	recess	zero
cycle	flavor	locate	require	
decay	frozen	major		

VC-CV/CLOSED SYLLABLE WORDS

admit	fifteen	lancer	plastic	tennis
appoint	foggy	letter	problem	tractor
ballad	follow	lumber	public	traffic
bamboo	ginger	master	quagmire	trigger
bandit	goblin	member	question	tunnel
better	gossip	metric	quitter	ulcer
bonnet	hobby	motto	rascal	umpire
cactus	hollow	muffin	rescue	under
candy	ignite	napkin	robber	upper
cotton	imbed	nectar	rubber	vampire
daddy	index	number	silver	velvet
dentist	issue	nutmeg	splendid	victor
disgust	jelly	object	splinter	welcome
doctor	jobber	offer	suffer	western
dummy	justice	optic	summer	whisper
effort	kennel	picnic	supper	window
endure	kitten	pillow	tamper	yellow
fancy	ladder	pistol	temper	yonder
				zipper

-LE WORDS/CLOSED SYLLABLE

amble	dibble	kindle	rattle	stubble
ample	dimple	knuckle	riddle	stumble
angle	dingle	little	ripple	subtle
ankle	dribble	mangle	rubble	suckle
apple	drizzle	mantle	ruffle	supple
babble	dwindle	meddle	rumble	tackle
baffle	fickle	middle	rumple	tangle
bangle	fiddle	mingle	saddle	tattle
battle	fizzle	mottle	sample	temple
bobble	fondle	muddle	scribble	thimble
bottle	frazzle	muffle	scuffle	thistle
bramble	freckle	mumble	scuttle	throttle
brindle	frizzle	muscle	settle	tickle
bristle	fumble	muzzle	shackle	tingle
brittle	gamble	nestle	shingle	tipple
bubble	gentle	nettle	shuffle	topple
buckle	giggle	nibble	shuttle	trample
bundle	gobble	niggle	sickle	tremble
bungle	grapple	nimble	simple	trestle
bustle	griddle	nipple	single	trickle
cackle	grumble	nozzle	sizzle	truckle
candle	haggle	nuzzle	smuggle	truffle
castle	handle	paddle	snaffle	trundle
cattle	heckle	pebble	sniffle	tumble
chuckle	bobble	pestle	snuffle	twiddle
cobble	huddle	pickle	snuggle	twinkle
cockle	humble	piddle	spangle	uncle
coddle	hustle	pimple	sparkle	wabble
crackle	jangle	prattle	spindle	waddle
cripple	jiggle	prickle	spittle	waffle
crumble	jingle	puddle	sprinkle	waggle
crumple	joggle	puzzle	squiggle	whittle
cuddle	jostle	quibble	stickle	wimple
dabble	juggle	rabble	straddle	wiggle
dangle	jumble	raffle	strangle	wrangle
dapple	jungle	ramble	straggler	wrestle
dazzle	kettle	rankle	struggle	wrinkle
				wriggle

-LE WORDS/OPEN SYLLABLE

able	cable	gable	sable	stifle
beadle	cradle	idle	scruple	table
beagle	cycle	ladle	sidle	title
beetle	eagle	maple	stable	treacle
bridle	fable	people	staple	trifle
bugle	feeble	rifle	steeple	wheedle

a-, ab- (away from)

abide
abloom
abnormal
abode
abound

ante- (before)

antecede
antechamber
antenatal
antepenult
anteroom
antetype

anti- (against)

antibacterial
antibody
anticatalyst
anticlerical
antifreeze
antitank
antitoxin
antiwar

auto- (self)

autobiography
autobus
autoharp
autohypnosis
automobile

bi- (two)

bicycle
bimetal
bimonthly
bipolar
biweekly

circu- (around)

circumnavigate
circumpolar
circumscribe

co- (together, with)

cobelligerants
coefficient
coexist
cohabit
coheir

counter- (against)

counteract
counterattack
counterbalance
counterclaim
counterculture
counterrevolution
counterspy
counterweight

de- (away, down)

deactivate
debar
debase
debrief
decamp
degrade
dehumidify
delouse

dis- (apart from, not)

disallow
disappoint
disarm
discontinue
discount
discredit
disenchant
dislocate
disobey

ex- (from)

excogitate
excommunicate
exfoliate
exsanguinate

extra- (outside, beyond)

extracurricular
extragalactic
extrajudical
extralegal
extraordinary
extrasensory
extraterritorial

fore- (in front)

forearm
forebode
forecastle
forefinger
forefoot
forefront
foreground
forehand
forehead
foremast

PREFIXES

il- (not)
illegal
illegible
illiterate
illogical

im- (not)
immaterial
immature
immeasurable
imperfect
impersonal
impolite
improper
impure

in- (not)
inaccessible
inactive
inarticulate
inclement
incomplete
inconvenient
independent
indifferent
indirect
insane

inter- (between, among)
interact
intercede
interchange
intercontinental
intermingle
intermix
intersection
interstellar

ir- (not)
irradiate
irrational
irregular
irrelevant
irreligious
irreplaceable
irrepressable
irresponsible
irreverent
irreversible

mid- (middle)
midair
midday
midland
midnight
midpoint
midships
midsummer

mis- (wrong)
misadventure
misapply
miscast
miscue
misfortune
misname
misspell
misstep
misunderstand

non- (not)
nonabrasive
nonburnable
nonconductor
nondurable
nonentity
nonsmoker
nonviolent
nonvocal
nonvoter
nonunion

over- (over)
overactive
overbold
overcharge
overdress
overgrown
overlay
overpay
overreact
overrun
overtax

post- (after)
postdate
postoperative
postscript
postwar

pre- (before)
precaution
preclude
precursor
predate
predict
prefabricate
prefix
premarital
prepay
presume

pro- (before, in front, forward, forth)
procreate
produce
profess
profile
profound
project
pronoun
provoke

re- (again)
reclaim
redo
refinish
reline
relive
remount
repaint
replace

sub- (under)
subdivide
submarine
subnormal
subplot
subsoil
substandard
suburban

super- (over)
supercede
supercharge
superego
superhighway
superhuman
superman
supernatural
supermarket
supernova

tele- (far away)
telegram
telegraph
telephone
telephoto
telescope
television

trans- (across)
translucent
transmigrate
transplant
transpolar
transport
transpose

un- (not)
unclear
uneven
unfair
unfit
unglue
unhook
unlace
unlock
unpack
untie
untouched

uni- (one)
unicellular
unicycle
unilateral

SUFFIXES

-able (tending to, able to)	-age (state of being) (place of, result of)	-al (relating to)	-ance, -ence (state of being)	-ary, -ery (that which, place where)
conquerable	anchorage	commercial	allowance	bakery
enjoyable	orphanage	electrical	attendance	cannery
lovable	parsonage	residential	difference	creamery
payable	personage	technical	excellence	dictionary
perishable	shrinkage	theatrical	importance	forgery
readable	wastage			nursery
reliable				revolutionary
washable				

-en (having nature of)	-en (to make or become)	-er (one who, that which)	-er (more "in degree")	-est (most "in degree")
ashen	blacken	baker	faster	cleanest
broken	fatten	carpenter	fatter	deepest
earthen	flatten	cleaner	lighter	easiest
fallen	lengthen	foreigner	nicer	farthest
golden	roughen	grocer	sicker	latest
molten	shorten	jumper	shorter	longest
spoken	straighten	preacher	slower	loudest
swollen	whiten	runner	smarter	skinniest
wooden	widen	teacher	stronger	tightest
woven		worker	taller	widest

-ful (characterized by, full of)	-fy (make or form into)	-hood (state of rank)	-ic (pertaining to, like)
		adulthood	
awful	clarify	boyhood	angelic
beautiful	glorify	brotherhood	artistic
graceful	horrify	childhood	athletic
helpful	identify	falsehood	atmospheric
masterful	justify	maidenhood	classic
plentiful	modify	manhood	critic
skillful	notify	neighborhood	dramatic
successful	qualify	priesthood	historic
thankful	simplify	womanhood	volcanic
wonderful	testify		

-ive
(having nature of quality of, given to)

active
corrective
destructive
effective
explosive
festive
impressive
inventive
protective

-ity, -ty
(state of being)

acidity
purity
reality
sovereignty

-ist
(one who)

artist
biologist
botonist
communist
humorist
journalist
loyalist
optomist
pessimist
pianist

-ish
(having nature of)

bluish
childish
clownish
fiendish
foolish
sickish
sixish
whitish

-less
(without)

ageless
childless
fatherless
graceless
helpless
hopeless
merciless
penniless
priceless
witless
worthless

-ly
(in the manner of)

actively
attentively
happily
justly
patiently
quietly
rapidly
sadly
silently
swiftly

-ment
(resulting state, action or process)

amazement
commitment
employment
movement
payment
placement
punishment
refinement
settlement
treatment

-most
(most "in degree")

aftermost
bottommost
foremost
furthermost
hindmost
innermost
northernmost
outermost
topmost

-ness
(quality or state of being)

blindness
gladness
goodness
kindness
likeness
sickness
sweetness
thickness
weakness
wickedness

-or
(person who, state of quality)

actor
auditor
creditor
debtor
executor
supervisor

-ous
(state or condition, having quality of)

courageous
dangerous
humorous
joyous
nervous
prosperous

-ship
(office, profession art, or skill)

championship
fellowship
friendship
hardship
horsemanship
marksmanship
partnership
penmanship
relationship
sportsmanship

-tion, -ion
(act, process, state)

action
attraction
collection
correction
dictation
education
election
narration
protection
rejection

-ure
(act, process)

adventure
composure
enclosure
failure
pleasure

CONTRACTIONS

aren't	she'd	
can't	she'll	
couldn't	she's	
didn't	shouldn't	
doesn't	that's	
don't	there's	
hadn't	they'd	
hasn't	they'll	
haven't	they're	
he'd	wasn't	
he'll	we'd	
he's	we'll	
here's	we're	
I'd	weren't	
I'll	what's	
I'm	where's	
isn't	who'd	
it's	who's	
I've	won't	
let's	wouldn't	
mustn't	you'll	
	you're	
	you've	

PREPOSITIONS

about
above
across
after
along
among
amongst
around
as
at
before
behind
below
beside
between
by
down
for
from
in
inside
into
like
of
off
on
onto
out
outside
over
through
to
toward
under
underneath
until
up
upon
with
within

CONJUNCTIONS

Co-ordinating

and
but
for
nor
or
so
yet

Subordinating

after
because
if
since
till
when
where
while

36

COMPOUND WORDS

afternoon
airline
airplane
alongside
anybody
anyone
anyplace
anything
anytime
anyway
anywhere
arrowhead
backbone
backyard
baseball
baseman
basketball
bathrobe
bathroom
bathtub
bedroom
bedtime
beehive
birdbath
blackboard
blacksmith
boathouse
boldface
broomstick
buckskin
businessmen
butterfly
campfire
campground
candlestick
cannot
catfish
chairman
chalkboard
checkerboard
cheeseburger
classmate
classroom
coastline
coffeepot
commonplace
corncob
cornfield

countryman
countryside
courthouse
courtyard
cowboy
craftsman
crossbow
daybreak
daytime
dishpan
doorbell
doorway
downhill
downstairs
downstream
downtown
driftwood
driveway
drugstore
dugout
earthquake
eggshell
elsewhere
everybody
everyday
everyone
everything
everywhere
eyebrow
eyelid
farewell
farmhouse
farmland
fingerprint
fireman
firewood
fireworks
flagpole
flashlight
flowerpot
football
footprint
footstep
forget
framework
freshman
furthermore
gingerbread

goldfish
grandfather
grandmother
grasshopper
grassland
hairbrush
halfway
handkerchief
handshake
handwriting
headdress
headline
highlands
highway
hillside
homeland
homemade
homework
hopscotch
horseback
horseman
horseshoe
hourglass
houseboat
household
housewife
however
icebox
indoor
inland
inside
intake
into
junkyard
landmark
landowner
lifetime
lighthouse
lightweight
limestone
lookout
lowlands
mailbox
mainland
moonlight
mountainside

newspaper
nightfall
nobody
northeast
northwest
notebook
nothing
nowhere
offspring
otherwise
outcome
outdoors
outline
outside
overall
overcome
overhead
overlook
overnight
paintbrush
pancake
playground
policeman
popcorn
proofread
quarterback
raincoat
raindrop
rainfall
railroad
railway
rattlesnake
roadside
rowboat
runaway
runway

sailboat
salesman
sandstone
scarecrow
schoolhouse
schoolroom
scrapbook
seaport
seashell
seashore
seaweed
sidewalk
snowball
snowflake
snowman
somebody
someday
somehow
someone
something
sometime
somewhat
somewhere
southeast
southwest
spaceship
springtime
stagecoach
stairway
starfish
steamboat
storekeeper
suitcase
summertime
sundown
sunlight
sunrise
sunset
sunshine

textbook
themselves
thereafter
throughout
townspeople
treetop
typewriter
undergo
underground
underline
underlying
underside
understand
underwater
upright
upstream
vineyard
warehouse
waterfall
waterway
weekend
whatever
whenever
whereas
wherever
whoever
widespread
wildlife
windmill
withdraw
within
without
woodland
worthwhile
yourself

A.D.	Anno Domini, in the year of our Lord	elem.	elementary
ad., adv.	advertisement	enc.	enclosure
A.M., a.m.	ante meridiem, before noon	enc.	encyclopedia
Amer.	America; American	Eng.	English
anon.	anonymous	Esq.	Esquire
apt.	apartment	E.S.T.	Eastern Standard Time
assn.	association	etc.	et cetera, and so forth
assoc.	associate; associated	F	Fahrenheit
asst.	assistant	FBI	Federal Bureau of Investigation
atty.	attorney	FDA	Food and Drug Administration
ave.	avenue	fig.	figure
B.A.	Bachelor of Arts	Fr.	Father; Friar; French
B.C.	Before Christ; British Columbia	Fri.	Friday
bibliog.	bibliography	ft.	feet; foot; fort
bldg.	building	gal.	gallon
blvd.	boulevard	geog.	geography
bros.	brothers	Gov.	Governor
bur.	bureau	govt.	government
C	Centigrade; Celcius	grad.	graduate; graduated
cal.	calories	gr.	gram
cap.	capital	hdqrs.	headquarters
cdr.	commander	Heb.	Hebrew; Hebrews
cent.	century	hist.	historical; history
ch., chap.	chapter	Hon.	Honorable
chm.	chairman	ht.	height; heat
cm.	centimeter	I., i.	island
c/o	care of	ibid.	ibidem, in the same place
co.	company; county	ill., illus.	illustration
c.o.d.	cash on delivery collect on delivery	inc.	incorporated; including
coll.	college; collection	in.	inch
conf.	conference	incog.	incognito (unknown)
Cont.	Continental	Ind.	Indian; Indiana
cont.	continued	ins.	insurance
coop.	cooperative	int.	interest; international
cop, ©	copyright	intro.	introduction
corp.	corporation	I.O.U.	I owe you
C.S.T.	Central Standard Time	I.Q.	intelligence quotient
D.A.	District Attorney	Jr.	Junior
DDT	dichloro-diphenyl-trichloroethane	junc.	junction
Dem.	Democrat	kg.	kilogram
dept.	department	km.	kilometer
diag.	diagram	l.	liter
dict.	dictionary	lab.	laboratory
dm.	decimeter	lang.	language
doz.	dozen	lat.	latitude
Dr.	doctor	lb.	pound
D.S.T.	Daylight Saving Time	leg.	legislature
ed.	edition	lib.	librarian; library
educ.	education	liq.	liquid
		lit.	literature
		Lt., Lieut.	Lieutenant

SELECTED ABBREVIATIONS

Ltd., Lim.	Limited	Prof.	Professor
m.	meter	prop.	property
M.A.	Master of Arts	Prov.	Proverbs
math	mathematics	P.S.	post scriptum, postscript
max.	maximum	P.S.T.	Pacific Standard Time
M.D.	Doctor of Medicine	pt.	pint
mdse.	merchandise	qt.	quart
meas.	measure	rd.	road
memo	memorandum	recd.	received
mfg.	manufacturing	ref.	reference; refer
mfr., manuf.	manufacturer	reg.	region; regulation
min.	minute	regt.	regiment
misc.	miscellaneous	rep.	representative; republic
Mlle.	Mademoiselle	Rev.	Reverend; Revelations
mi.	mile	rev.	review; revise; revolution
mml.	millimeter	R.I.P.	rest in peace
Mme.	Madame	R.R.	railroad
mo.	month	R.S.V.P.	Answer, if you please
Mon.	Monday	Ry.	railway
mph	miles per hour	Sat.	Saturday
Msgr.	Monsignor	sch.	school
Mr.	Mister	sec.	second
Mrs.	Mistress	secy.	secretary
M.S.T.	Mountain Standard Time	sig.	signature
Mt., mt.	Mount; mountain	sing.	singular
mun.	municipal	sp.	spelling; species; space
myth	mythology	spec.	specification
n.	noun; north	sq.	square
nat., natl.	national	Sr.	Senior
NATO	North Atlantic Treaty Organization	St.	Saint; strait; street
		subj.	subject
no.	number	Sun.	Sunday
O.K.	correct; all right	Supt.	Superintendent
oz.	ounce	syn.	synonym
p.	page	t.	ton
par.	paragraph; parenthesis	tech.	technical; technology
parl.	parliament	temp.	temperature
pat.	patent	Thurs.	Thursday
pd.	paid	treas.	treasurer
per cent	per centum	Tues.	Tuesday
Ph.D.	Doctor of Philosophy	UN	United Nations
philos.	philosophy	univ.	university
phot., photog.	photograph	v.	verb
pk.	park; peak; peck	v, vs	versus, against
pl.	plural; place; plate	vet.	veteran; veterinary
P.M., p.m.	post meridiem, after noon; postmaster; post mortem	VIP	Very Important Person
		vol.	volume
P.O.	post office	V.P.	Vice-President
pop.	population	Wed.	Wednesday
POW	prisoner of war	wk.	week
ppd.	prepaid	wt.	weight
Pres.	President	Xmas	Christmas
prin.	principal	yd.	yard
		yr.	year

SELECTED WORD LIST

Word	Synonym	Antonym	Homonym
above	over	below	—
absent	missing	present	—
abuse	mistreat	abet	—
add	total	subtract	—
adept	proficient	unskilled	—
adore	love	hate	—
advance	proceed	retreat	—
aid	help	hinder	ade, aide
air	atmosphere	earth	heir
aisle	passageway	blockade	isle
alike	same	different	—
all	everything	none	awl
alter	change	preserve	—
ancient	old	modern	—
answer	reply	question	—
appear	emerge	disappear	—
arid	dry	wet	—
ate	consumed	fasted	eight
attach	fasten	remove	—
aunt	—	—	ant
awake	arouse	asleep	—
baby	infant	adult	—
back	rear	front	—
backward	reversed	forward	—
bad	evil	good	—
bag	sack	box	—
bare	naked	clothed	bear
basis	foundation	summit	bases
be	exist	isn't	bee
beach	shore	ocean	beech
beat	rhythm	—	beet
beautiful	lovely	ugly	—
been	was	wasn't	bin
before	formerly	after	—
begin	start	end	—
below	beneath	above	—
bend	curve	straighten	—
black	dark	white	—
blew	gusted	calmed	blue
blunt	dull	sharp	—
boat	ship	—	—
bore	weary	excite	boar
*bow	submit	refuse	bough
bowl	dish	—	bole, boll
box	carton	—	—
brave	courageous	frightened	—
break	shatter	repair	brake
breath	respiration	—	breadth
bridal	wedding	—	bridle
bright	brilliant	dim	—
brink	edge	center	—
bury	inter	unearth	berry
buy	purchase	sell	by, bye
calm	tranquil	excited	—

*heteronym

41

Word	Synonym	Antonym	Homonym
canvas	fabric	paper	—
cap	hat	—	—
capital	wealth	liability	capitol
caret	insertion	deletion	carot, carrot
carpet	rug	—	—
cereal	porridge	—	serial
chief	leader	follower	—
city	metropolis	country	—
choose	select	reject	—
clever	smart	dumb	—
*close	shut	open	—
coarse	rough	smooth	course
cold	icy	hot	—
collect	gather	disperse	—
come	arrive	go	—
comic	funny	tragic	—
compliment	praise	criticise	complement
cool	chilly	warm	—
counsel	advise	ignore	council
creek	brook	—	creak
cry	weep	laugh	—
damage	injure	repair	—
danger	peril	safety	—
dark	opaque	light	—
day	daylight	night	—
dead	deceased	alive	—
dear	darling	—	deer
decrease	reduce	increase	—
deep	great	shallow	—
*desert	abandon	retrieve	dessert
despise	hate	adore	—
devour	eat	regurgitate	—
die	decease	live	dye
difficult	hard	easy	—
dirty	filthy	clean	—
disperse	distribute	gather	—
distant	far	near	—
dry	arid	wet	—
dull	boring	exciting	—
early	premature	late	—
elusive	evasive	overt	—
eminent	prominent	obscure	—
employ	hire	fire	—
empty	vacant	full	—
end	finish	begin	—
enemy	foe	friend	—
enlarge	expand	reduce	—
entice	tempt	scorn	—
error	mistake	truth	—
even	—	odd	—
exceed	excel	fail	—
except	but	—	—

*heteronym

42

SELECTED WORD LIST

Word	Synonym	Antonym	Homonym
excess	overabundance	lack	—
exit	leave	enter	—
expand	swell	contract	—
export	send	import	—
fail	flop	succeed	—
fair	just	unfair	fare
fall	descend	rise	—
fat	obese	thin	—
feat	deed	—	fete
feeble	weak	strong	—
first	foremost	last	—
fix	repair	break	—
flower	blossom	—	flour
forth	forward	back	fourth
form	shape	unformed	—
follow	pursue	lead	—
foolish	silly	wise	—
formerly	before	after	—
frighten	terrify	soothe	—
funny	humorous	serious	—
fur	pelt	—	fir
future	hereafter	past	—
gain	profit	loss	—
gamble	bet	—	gambol
gather	assemble	disburse	—
gaunt	thin	plump	—
gaze	stare	glance	—
generous	magnanimous	selfish	—
gift	present	—	—
giggle	chuckle	whimper	—
good	kind	bad	—
gorilla	ape	—	—
great	large	small	grate
groan	moan	laugh	grown
hail	—	—	hell
halt	stop	advance	—
hangar	shed	—	hanger
happy	glad	sad	—
hard	rigid	soft	—
hare	rabbit	—	hair
harmless	safe	detrimental	—
hate	despise	love	—
heal	cure	infect	heel
healthy	well	ill	—
heavy	weighty	light	—
here	present	there	hear
heroine	victor	loser	heroin
hinder	obstruct	help	—
holy	sacred	profane	wholly
homely	ugly	pretty	—
hot	heated	cold	—
huge	large	tiny	—

*heteronym

43

Word	Synonym	Antonym	Homonym
hurl	throw	catch	—
idle	slothful	busy	idol, idyll
ill	sick	well	—
illusive	phantasmal	tangible	—
imaginary	illusory	real	—
in	inside	out	inn
inflate	expand	deflate	—
iniquity	wickedness	goodness	—
innocent	faultless	guilty	—
insight	discernment	—	incite
its	—	—	it's
joy	happiness	sadness	—
keen	sharp	blunt	—
knave	rascal	gentleman	nave
knows	understands	(is) ignorant	nose
latch	lock	unbolt	—
late	tardy	early	—
leak	crack	—	leek
leave	depart	return	—
led	guided	followed	*lead
liar	deceiver	—	lyre
like	same	different	—
*live	exist	die	—
little	small	big	—
lone	one	several	loan
loose	free	tight	—
loud	noisy	quiet	—
low	inferior	high	lo
made	created	destroyed	maid
male	man	—	mail
mantle	cloak	—	mantel
medal	award	—	metal, mettle
meet	assemble	adjourn	meat
minor	petty	major	—
missle	projectile	—	missal
more	additional	less	—
mourning	grief	gladness	morning
mousse	—	—	moose
muscle	strength	weakness	mussel
narrow	limited	wide	—
native	indigenous	foreign	—
natural	normal	strange	—
naval	nautical	—	navel
neat	orderly	disarrayed	—
necessary	obligatory	unnecessary	—
need	require	have	knead
new	contemporary	old	knew, gnu
night	evening	day	—
no	negative	yes	know
noisy	loud	quiet	—
none	nothing	all	nun
not	—	—	knot
open	unfasten	close	—
our	—	—	hour

*heteronym

Word	Synonym	Antonym	Homonym
pain	ache	pleasure	pane
pair	twins	single	pare
pale	pallid	rosy	pail
pallet	—	—	palette, palate
peace	accord	war	piece
peal	ring	—	peel
pin	fasten	undo	—
place	put	remove	plaice
plain	intelligible	confusing	plane
polite	courteous	rude	—
powerful	strong	weak	—
presence	proximity	absence	*presents
prey	quarry	hunter	pray
principle	essential	unnecessary	principal
prohibit	forbid	permit	—
*project	protrude	recede	—
push	shove	pull	—
question	query	answer	—
raise	elevate	lower	raze
*read	peruse	—	reed
real	actual	fake	reel
*record	chronicle	play	—
red	florid	pale	read
*refuse	decline	accept	—
reign	rule	obey	rain
remain	stay	leave	—
rich	wealthy	poor	—
right	correct	wrong	wright, rite
ring	peal	—	wring
rock	stone	—	—
rode	drove	walked	road
rough	coarse	smooth	ruff
route	course	—	root, rout
rumor	gossip	truth	roomer
sad	unhappy	glad	—
same	identical	different	—
scene	setting	—	seen
scents	smells	—	cents
scream	yell	whisper	—
sea	ocean	—	see
seem	appear	is	seam
sell	vend	purchase	cell
sent	dispatched	returned	—
serf	slave	master	surf
sheer	thin	opaque	shear
shop	store	—	—
shy	timid	aggressive	—
sight	vision	blindness	site, cite
slay	murder	save	sleigh
sleep	slumber	wake	—
slow	dilatory	fast	sloe
small	tiny	large	—
smile	grin	frown	—
soar	fly	land	sore

*heteronym

45

SELECTED WORD LIST

Word	Synonym	Antonym	Homonym
sole	only	several	soul
some	few	many	sum
son	scion	—	sun
sour	acerbic	sweet	—
*sow	plant	reap	so, sew
speak	talk	listen	—
stake	peg	—	steak
stare	gaze	glance	stair
start	begin	stop	—
stationary	motionless	movable	stationery
steal	rob	buy	steel
straight	undeviating	curved	strait
stray	deviate	stay	—
strong	substantial	weak	—
stubborn	obstinate	yielding	—
tacks	nails	—	tax
take	steal	return	—
tale	fable	—	tail
tardy	late	punctual	—
taught	instructed	learned	taut
tea	—	—	tee
*tear	—	—	tier
there	—	here	their, they're
threw	pitched	caught	through
time	—	—	thyme
timid	afraid	assured	—
to	—	from	too, two
top	apex	bottom	—
tow	pull	push	toe
troupe	company	—	troop
true	certain	false	—
unique	original	common	—
usual	normal	rare	—
vacant	empty	full	—
vain	futile	warranted	vein, vane
vice	fault	virtue	—
wait	tarry	rush	weight
want	desire	need	won't
waste	squander	conserve	waist
wave	bellow	—	waive
way	direction	—	weigh
weak	feeble	strong	week
wear	don	—	where
well	fortuitous	ill	—
*wind	breeze	—	—
whole	entire	—	hole
whose	—	—	who's
wild	savage	tame	—
whoa	stop	go	woe
wood	lumber	—	would
won	succeeded	lost	one
wry	crooked	straight	rye
you	—	—	ewe, yew

*heteronym

46

She bawled her eyes out.
My brother gets in my hair.
He lost his marbles.
The idea rang a bell.
He was burned up.
Go fly a kite.
He almost bit my head off!
She blew her stack.
He's on top of the world.
She is as quiet as a church mouse.
He's as neat as a pin.
The baby is prettier than a picture.
He's like a bull in a china shop.
He is as ugly as a mud fence.
Money was as scarce as hen's teeth.
That will take him down a peg.
Dad will get wind of it.
Money always burns a hole in my pocket.
Will you lend me a hand?
She was so nervous she blew the test.
I was so scared, I was shaking in my boots.
The girl was walking on air after the dance.
I was furious, but I held my tongue.
I'm between the devil and the deep blue sea.
He's not worth a hill of beans.
I think he bit off more than he can chew.
It's raining cats and dogs out there!
He has a trick up his sleeve.
It's as plain as the nose on your face.
His father is well heeled.
I'm in a pretty pickle!
Do you have a skeleton in your closet?
The handwriting was on the wall.
She can really put on the dog.
He's a stool pigeon for the police.

I'm coming, so keep your shirt on.
He's tied to his mother's apron strings.
I'll stay until the bitter end.
He's talking through his hat.
That's right down my alley.
He is a pain in the neck.
The cowboy bit the dust.
He's as nutty as a fruitcake.
I have a splitting headache.
Put your John Hancock on the paper.
I never see eye to eye with you.
Is she ever in the dumps!
For crying out loud, stop that noise.
I have a bone to pick with you!
She really can chew the fat.
You just hit the nail on the head.
By hook or by crook I'll get it.
That rings a bell with me.
The judge will throw the book at him.
Don't get your dander up.
It's nothing to shake a stick at.
Hold your horses!
I just had to blow off steam.
Keep a stiff upper lip.
I believe she is full of beans.
The teacher called him on the carpet.
That is as easy as rolling off a log.
I've got to get forty winks.
He has too many irons in the fire.
It was a long row to hoe.
She's as mad as a wet hen.
It is not fake, it's the real McCoy.
You're in the doghouse now!
That is just a drop in the bucket.
The doctor says I'm fit as a fiddle.

After winning the lottery, I'll be on Easy Street.
The storekeeper wanted cash on the barrelhead.
I broke the window, and I'm in hot water now!
He bought the company and then lost his shirt.
After the accident, things were touch and go.
You have to make hay while the sun shines.
What I say to him goes in one ear and out the other.
Don't make a mountain out of a molehill.
I'll keep my eye on the baby for you.
The dead fish smelled to high heaven.
I saw the snake and almost jumped out of my skin.
She surely goes hog wild getting a party ready.
We played a game at the party to break the ice.
To clean that dirty oven, I have to use lots of elbow grease.
He cried wolf one too many times.
Don't cry over spilt milk.
You're skating on thin ice when you tell your mother a lie.
Are you getting cold feet about asking for more money?
Many sailors have gone to Davy Jones's locker.
He got into the party by crashing the gate.
He's just trying to keep up with the Joneses.